Patricia Rind

Women's Best Friendships
Beyond Betty, Veronica,
Thelma, and Louise

*Pre-publication
REVIEWS,
COMMENTARIES,
EVALUATIONS . . .*

"This book brings back wonderful memories of best friendships in childhood and adulthood. Rind has compiled stories of best friends, interviewing women of different ages and backgrounds. The book depicts the intimacy, heartbreaks, trust, fun, and passion of girls and women making and keeping friends. It reminds us to cherish our female friends and prioritize them over other relationships."

Esther Rothblum, PhD
Editor, *Journal of Lesbian Studies;*
Professor of Psychology
and Director of Clinical Training,
University of Vermont,
Burlington

"Given the scientific evidence of the role of social support in psychological and physical health, it is important to understand how relationships are formed and utilized. Dr. Rind pro-

vides an in-depth look at one of the most powerful sources of social support—best friendships among women. *Women's Best Friendships* is scholarly in its method and colloquial in its presentation, making it accessible to any woman who seeks to understand her closest female friendships.

I found myself nodding in agreement many times during the course of reading this book. The participants' stories touched on many characteristics of women's friendships that I could relate to—from the discomfort of competitiveness to the deep contentment of 'being known' by a friend. I particularly enjoyed Dr. Rind's reflections on the interview material. These passages offered a thought-provoking analysis of the individual stories and an integration of the work of relevant theorists and researchers. I am appreciative of Dr. Rind for providing such a detailed, inside look at women's best friendships. I am looking forward to sharing this book with my best friend!"

Sally J. Wendt, PhD
Assistant Professor of Psychology,
Marymount College,
Tarrytown, NY

"*Women's Best Friendships: Beyond Betty, Veronica, Thelma, and Louise* is a delightful and engaging set of stories about the best friendships of seven heterosexual women who differ in age, marital status, and race. The focus on women's friendships is designed to fill a gap in our cultural and scientific understanding of this very important and frequently neglected aspect of women's relationships. Based on the author's doctoral dissertation, the stories are told and analyzed according to qualitative research traditions. The themes identified in these friendships include those having to do with the meaningfulness of being known by another and struggles with feelings of competition and dependency.

Reading these stories and thematic analyses is an evocative experience that not only illuminates the best friendships of these seven women, but also sheds light on one's own history and pattern of female friendships. One cannot help but compare one's own experience with female friendships to the rich and complex array of relationships presented in this book. As such, this book is both a contribution to the research literature on women's relationships, as well as a good companion for all women whose lives are enriched and strengthened by significant female friendships. Most important, the focus on women's friendships promotes the kind of valuing of these relationships that cannot help but enhance women's lives."

Mary Sue Richardson, PhD
Professor, Department
of Applied Psychology,
New York University

"*Without either glorifying or pathologizing, Patricia Rind shares with us the stories of seven heterosexual women's best friendships with other women, and the ways these friendships are 'woven' into the interviewees' lives. In sharing these stories, and through Rind's own analyses of the themes embedded in them, the reader is able to 'feel with' the women the complex pushes and pulls of their intimate female friendships as these friendships develop within the context of the women's lives, personalities, and relational needs and styles. We experience the dialectical tensions of connection and competition, independence and dependence, knowing and being known, and we watch the women themselves struggle with these tensions even as they reflect upon the aspects of the best friendships they most appreciate.

Rind takes a unique approach to the study of women's friendships, relying on interviewees' stories of their friendships and the author's own reflections upon these stories in relation to each other, the literature on women's relational styles, and her own experiences and perspectives on women's friendships. Taken together, these stories and Rind's interpretations of them help to convey the depth and complexity of connection in women's friendships; in so doing, they serve as a necessary counter to the typically superficial portrayals of women's friendships in the media."

Jacqueline S. Weinstock, PhD
Assistant Professor,
University of Vermont,
Human Development
and Family Studies Program

Women's Best Friendships
Beyond Betty, Veronica, Thelma, and Louise

HAWORTH Innovations in Feminist Studies
J. Dianne Garner
Senior Editor

New, Recent, and Forthcoming Titles:

God's Country: A Case Against Theocracy by Sandy Rapp

Women and Aging: Celebrating Ourselves by Ruth Raymond Thone

Women's Conflicts About Eating and Sexuality: The Relationship Between Food and Sex by Rosalyn M. Meadow and Lillie Weiss

A Woman's Odyssey into Africa: Tracks Across a Life by Hanny Lightfoot-Klein

Anorexia Nervosa and Recovery: A Hunger for Meaning by Karen Way

Women Murdered by the Men They Loved by Constance A. Bean

Reproductive Hazards in the Workplace: Mending Jobs, Managing Pregnancies by Regina Kenen

Our Choices: Women's Personal Decisions About Abortion by Sumi Hoshiko

Tending Inner Gardens: The Healing Art of Feminist Psychotherapy by Lesley Irene Shore

The Way of the Woman Writer by Janet Lynn Roseman

Racism in the Lives of Women: Testimony, Theory, and Guides to Anti-Racist Practice by Jeanne Adleman and Gloria Enguídanos

Advocating for Self: Women's Decisions Concerning Contraception by Peggy Matteson

Feminist Visions of Gender Similarities and Differences by Meredith M. Kimball

Experiencing Abortion: A Weaving of Women's Words by Eve Kushner

Menopause, Me and You: The Sound of Women Pausing by Ann M. Voda

Fat—A Fate Worse Than Death?: Women, Weight, and Appearance by Ruth Raymond Thone

Feminist Theories and Feminist Psychotherapies: Origins, Themes, and Variations by Carolyn Zerbe Enns

Celebrating the Lives of Jewish Women: Patterns in a Feminist Sampler edited by Rachel Josefowitz Siegel and Ellen Cole

Women and AIDS: Negotiating Safer Practices, Care, and Representation edited by Nancy L. Roth and Linda K. Fuller

A Menopausal Memoir: Letters from Another Climate by Anne Herrmann

Women in the Antarctic edited by Esther D. Rothblum, Jacqueline S. Weinstock, and Jessica F. Morris

Breasts: The Women's Perspective on an American Obsession by Carolyn Latteier

Lesbian Stepfamilies: An Ethnography of Love by Janet M. Wright

Women, Families, and Feminist Politics: A Global Exploration by Kate Conway-Turner and Suzanne Cherrin

Women's Work: A Survey of Scholarship By and About Women edited by Donna Musialowski Ashcraft

Love Matters: A Book of Lesbian Romance and Relationships by Linda Sutton

Birth As a Healing Experience: The Emotional Journey of Pregnancy Through Postpartum by Lois Halzel Freedman

Unbroken Homes: Single-Parent Mothers Tell Their Stories by Wendy Anne Paterson

Transforming the Disciplines: A Women's Studies Primer edited by Elizabeth L. MacNabb, Mary Jane Cherry, Susan L. Popham, and René Perry Prys

Women at the Margins: Neglect, Punishment, and Resistance edited by Josephina Figueira-McDonough and Rosemary C. Sarri

Women's Best Friendships: Beyond Betty, Veronica, Thelma, and Louise by Patricia Rind

Women's Best Friendships
Beyond Betty, Veronica, Thelma, and Louise

Patricia Rind

The Haworth Press®
New York • London • Oxford

The Haworth Press, Inc., 10 Alice Street, Binghamton, NY 13904-1580.

Client identities and circumstances have been changed to protect confidentiality.

Cover design by Marylouise E. Doyle.

Library of Congress Cataloging-in-Publication Data

Rind, Patricia
    Women's best friendships : beyond Betty, Veronica, Thelma, and Louise / Patricia Rind.
        p. cm.
    Includes bibliographical references and index.
    ISBN 0-7890-1539-0 (alk. paper) — ISBN 0-7890-1540-4 (pbk. : alk. paper)
    1. Female friendships. I. Title.
BF575.F66 R56 2002
158.2'5'082—dc21

                                                    2002068755

For Michael, my love

ABOUT THE AUTHOR

Patricia Rind, PhD, is a specialist in women's sexuality and psychology. She has published articles in *The Journal of Sex Research, Family Planning Perspectives,* and *International Family Planning Perspectives.* She has taught and co-taught undergraduate and graduate classes in human sexuality and qualitative research methods. Dr. Rind is currently working on a project in which she will explore aspects of female sexuality using qualitative methods. Her current professional affiliations are with the American Psychological Association and the Society for the Scientific Study of Sexuality. She currently conducts seminars for parents on talking to kids about sex and sexuality.

CONTENTS

Preface

Do not start. Do not blush. Let us admit in the privacy of our own society that these things sometimes happen. Sometimes women do like women.[1]

My mother tells a story about when we first moved to the house in which I grew up. I was around four at the time. Apparently, along with all the disarray that accompanies moving, my mother had to contend with my continually crying to her that I needed a friend. I can imagine my mother, younger than I am now, shy and phone phobic, dreading the idea of having to call her real estate agent for the number of someone with a child my age, but understanding my apparent desperation. She somehow made that call and the next one, and got me a friend—a girl who became my best friend throughout my youth.

Many of my childhood memories are inseparable from that friendship. One of the things I remember most is that we wore the label "best friends" as if it were immutable. People at school and at the YWCA, where we took various lessons together, knew that we were best friends—and we knew they knew. There was an understanding that we could be friends with others, but that no one else could take on that role of best friend. What did that knowledge give us? I would imagine we felt happier and more confident knowing that whatever else we might have to deal with, we had each other. And if we made no other new friends, at least we were together. We understood each other. We played games that we made up and we shared confidences. We were teased by my older brother and we, in turn, teased her younger brother. We loved each other's families and walked in and out of each other's homes as if they were our own. We had minor disagreements and major fights, but we *had* to make up because we were best friends. I think there is a great deal of comfort in knowing, as perhaps only a child can, that a relationship will not change simply because you get angry with the other person.

For most of us, as we get older, our friendships change, as do the ways in which they develop. When we were children, the fact that another kid also liked her tuna sandwiches cut into triangles instead of squares could have been enough to spark a beautiful friendship. Although the roles that friends play might shift as we go through various stages of our life, we seem to find no less of a need for friendship when we are adults than when we are children searching for a playmate.

Close friendship between women has been a personal and academic interest of mine for some time. For as long as I can remember, there has been at least one girl or woman in my life whom I have called a best friend, although not always the same one. As I look back over those friendships, both the joy and the pain they have brought me are palpable. I have agonized over and reveled in these relationships to an extent only comparable to the relationships I have had with lovers.

Developing intimacy with another person can be extraordinarily exciting. I can remember an hours-long dinner with a friend that ended only because I had to catch a train. As we shared more and more of ourselves over the course of the evening, there seemed to be something akin to a magnetic force keeping us together. We had to actively pull ourselves apart—and back into the world of other people. On that train ride home, I remember feeling simultaneously exhilarated and drained. My body tingled with the excitement of having shared myself in ways I never had before.

On the flip side, I can think of nothing more hurtful than being betrayed by a close friend. To open yourself to another and then realize that she was not who you thought, can shake your very foundation. Losing an intense friendship can feel disorienting and earth-shattering, just as when a serious romantic relationship ends. It will likely require some grieving, as well as some time to evaluate your ability to judge character and to figure out how to structure your life around what can feel like a gaping hole.

I first started studying female friendship in graduate school. In my master's thesis, I examined female friendship in the novels of Mary Gordon and Gloria Naylor, as well as in the works of authors from an earlier period, including Edith Wharton and Jane Austen. At that time, my former college roommate, whom I have known since I was twelve, was my best friend, as she is to this day. Not long after I received my master's degree, I met another woman who has since become an extremely close friend. I have spent a good deal of time reflecting on the impact these two women have on my life. Although they are both extraordinarily important to me, my relationship with each is different.

I have known Jo-Ann since we were in the seventh grade, although we did not become very close until college, where we roomed together. We lived in the same city after college and were maids of honor at each other's weddings. Jo-Ann knows what I was like as a teenager and as a young adult. She saw the pain that my stuttering caused me as an adolescent. She was there as I fell in and out of love for the first time. Now, we are both married and have young children. She understands the difficulty in balancing work and family. I usually see her on weekends with our families—although we long for one-on-one time. I consider her a part of my extended family and I feel that I am a part of hers. Our friendship is continually getting deeper in ways that astound me. Jo-Ann knows how I got from there to here.

I met Ruth about twelve years ago at a job. We had an immediate connection and chemistry. Our sensibilities and senses of humor clicked right away. From the beginning, we could talk endlessly. We still do. We often find ourselves on the phone at one in the morning, winding up a three-hour conversation. Ruth and I understand each other, and when we don't, we discuss why not. I trust her in ways I trust no one else. Ruth challenges me to go ever deeper intellectually and emotionally. She also makes me laugh—usually at myself; sometimes she even makes me cry.

Considering the importance to me of my friendships with Jo-Ann and Ruth, it is probably not surprising that female friendship resurfaced once again as an area of interest. During my studies, I was surprised to learn that other researchers had just begun to scratch the surface of what I believed was a very significant facet of many women's lives. In addition, there seemed to be a pervasive notion that women were untrustworthy and competitive in their relationships with other women. In classes I have taught, I have been astounded to find college students, both male and female, holding onto the belief that women are sure to undermine their friendships when they are in pursuit of a man. Unfortunately, young girls are not taught that relationships with women outside their families are valuable. The stories we girls heard as we were growing up simply explained that ultimate happiness would be achieved when we married the man of our dreams and had his babies. Where were the movies, TV shows, and books emphasizing the amazing role women friends could play in one another's lives? I never read a fairy tale or saw a Disney movie that prepared me for the fact that my women friends would be woven so tightly into the fabric of my life—that they would be vital to my happiness and sense of well-being. Or, that to understand me, one had to understand how much I value my best friends.

During the course of my study, my two closest friends and friendships went through significant changes. First, Jo-Ann experienced the death of her baby daughter. Prior to this, I could not have imagined the level of anguish I felt for her during the following couple of years. That tragedy changed and deepened our friendship. As an amazing and painful coincidence, her daughter died on my older daughter's second birthday. The joy and sorrow of that date will forever be entwined for us both.

In the summer of 1996, while I was deep in the midst of my research, Ruth went abroad for several months. During that time we communicated primarily by e-mail, and through that medium we reached a depth of intimacy that, at times, surprised us both. She, too, has experienced a great deal of upheaval in her life since my research began. First, her grandmother, to whom she was very close, died. Soon after, her mother, who has a degenerative disease, became critically ill, which resulted in Ruth's premature return home. As a result of her mother's illness, Ruth's life was in almost constant turmoil for a few years. Once again, I shared in the suffering of a close friend.

When Jo-Ann's daughter died, I was faced with the knowledge that all of my love for her could do nothing to shield her from her pain. All I could do was call every day, see her whenever possible, and let her talk whenever she wanted. Late one night, when Ruth's mother was called in for a lung transplant and then informed it was not a match, all I could do once again was be there for her at the other end of the phone. I could not even be by her side at the hospital because of my own responsibilities at home. I agonized over my own limitations as a friend. Over time I came to understand, however, that my struggles with what I perceived as my shortcomings were only getting in the way of being the best friend I could be. Jo-Ann was not sitting around thinking about how I was falling short as a friend. Rather, she was mourning the death of her daughter and needed our time together to be about her.

These experiences, along with all my experiences of friendship, contributed to my understanding of the women's words contained in this book. I strongly believe that it is important to acknowledge and explain one's role in shaping the data. Who I am affected how I conducted interviews, the responses I received, and how I have chosen to present my findings. Very clearly, Jo-Ann's daughter's death provided me with a perspective on women's friendship that I did not have at the start of my study—one, needless to say, I would rather not have, but one that ultimately helped me to make better sense of some of the participants' stories I have included in these pages.

Acknowledgments

I thank most of all the women who participated in the study. I greatly appreciate their generosity of time and spirit.

This work came to fruition over three distinct phases. Throughout each, many people provided immeasurable help, advice, and support. The first phase, that of researching and writing the dissertation, was the longest and most arduous. I cannot imagine having completed my work without my colleagues at New York University, most important, Margot Ely, Suzanne Gabriele, Lisa Simon, and Niobe Way. In addition, Ruth Zlotnick somehow always found the time to read drafts of my work and offer insights. She has also been my most respected sounding board. All of these women, in varying ways, pushed me to think at a higher level.

Linda Chester and Meredith Phelan were the key players in the second phase—that of finding a publisher. Linda convinced me to get this book published, and Meredith provided enormous help in crafting my proposal. Wendy Brandes, true to her nature, provided a great deal of help, support, and advice during this period.

The final stage was, of course, the writing of this book. With enormous generosity, Diana Nolan did for me as a favor what she gets paid to do for others—she read, edited, proofread, and fine-tuned my work.

Thanks, too, to those who asked to read my dissertation and then talked to me about my work and about their best friendships. Those conversations kept me thinking in new ways. I also want to acknowledge the handful of girls and women who have been my best friends over the course of my life. They are all a part of this book.

My friendships with Jo-Ann Sternberg and Ruth Zlotnick provided the inspiration for my work. They both had to endure my in-depth analyses of our respective friendships over the years of this project. For not choosing to stick their fingers in their ears and sing the

"Star-Spangled Banner" instead of listen to me, I sincerely thank them. Both women mean the world to me.

The love and support of my mother, Ellin, my father, Ken, and my stepfather, Jim Fauvell, are forever and always invaluable. My brother, David, has always had confidence in me, even when I have lacked that confidence. Thanks must also go to Eileen Chieco for helping me to believe in myself.

In all my talk of best friendship, I sometimes may seem to fail to notice who is right beside me. That is not the case. It is through no accident that I have chosen to share my life with my husband, Michael. He provides a constant flow of love, laughter, and support, without which I would be lost. Karen and Rachel fill my days and my heart with love and joy.

Chapter 1

Introduction

Judging by the women I know, and judging by the success of popular books published on the subject—such as *Girlfriends,* by Carmen
Renee Berry and Tamara Traeder—women cherish the relationships
they have with their closest friends.[1] They say such things as, "I don't
know what I would do if she wasn't in my life" and "I know she'll be
there if I need her." These relationships are not assigned secondary
status in their lives. Yet, the relative quantity of research focusing on
women's other relationships could easily lead one to the mistaken
conclusion that women's best friends are far less tightly woven into
the fabric of their lives than are their lovers, children, and parents.

Although much has been written about friendship, in particular
comparing how men and women function within same-sex and cross-
sex friendships, only a handful of researchers have focused solely on
women's friendships. Of those, few have chosen to focus on the closest of those relationships, despite the fact that studies have, indeed,
shown the value women place on these friendships. Gouldner and
Strong found:

> To go without [a best] friend made some of the women feel that
> there was something lacking in their lives, that they were de-
> prived and were missing what they deserved to have. . . . Indeed,
> close friendship was thought of as the quintessential relation-
> ship, the unfettered tie that was entered into and pursued volun-
> tarily.[2]

Women's closest friendships are empowering. Contrary to the
popular notion that women's talk primarily involves "gossiping" and
"yakking," a friend's ability to listen in a noncritical fashion has been
found to bolster self-esteem and self-worth.[3] Furthermore, friendship
often enhances women's sense of autonomy and individuality. Indeed, friends provide support for independent pursuits, whereas

1

many husbands or male partners apparently discourage such activities.[4] Close friendships offer a sense of security that enables women to explore other interests and relationships outside of their family.

WOMEN AND FICTION

Historically, the roles that women have played in one another's lives have varied according to the cultural atmosphere of their time. Because fiction is so often a reflection of a period's cultural attitudes, beliefs, and circumstances, I believe it worthwhile to examine, albeit in a necessarily cursory fashion, some historical changes in the depictions of women's friendships by female novelists. It is vital to an understanding of women's friendships that we consider them in the cultural context in which they exist. Any examination of fictional literature written by women about women's friendship would be greatly wanting without the inclusion of Virginia Woolf's cleverly crafted chapter on fictional writer Mary Carmichael in *A Room of One's Own*. Woolf wrote of finding a book in a library about two women— Chloe and Olivia—who like each other:

> Chloe liked Olivia perhaps for the first time in literature. Cleopatra did not like Octavia. And how completely *Antony and Cleopatra* would have been altered had she done so! . . . And I tried to remember any case in the course of my reading where two women are represented as friends. . . . They are now and then mothers and daughters. But almost without exception they are shown in their relation to men.[5]

Woolf went on to explain that women have been written of only in relation to men—for example, as lovers, mothers, and daughters. What if men had been written of only in relation to women and "never [as] the friends of men, soldiers, thinkers, dreamers"? she asked. Her answer:

> We might perhaps have most of Othello; and a good deal of Antony; but no Caesar, no Brutus, no Hamlet, no Lear, no Jaques— literature would be incredibly impoverished, as indeed literature is impoverished beyond our counting by the doors that have been shut upon women.[6]

Thus, it was Woolf's contention that it is to the detriment of all that fiction had not depicted friendship between women. To never see women as they are in relation to other women, and to never explore their relationships, is to never understand so much of the richness— so many of the dimensions—of who they are.

Although this is clearly not the place to embark on a comprehensive survey of women writers' attitudes toward friendship, one may fairly contend that picking and choosing authors according to my fancy is not very, well, scientific. One might even argue that I have chosen novels and novelists to fit my hypotheses. Undoubtedly true, but it should also be noted that the books I have chosen to represent the early nineteenth century to the early twentieth century are three renowned works of that period: *Pride and Prejudice, Jane Eyre,* and *The House of Mirth.* Jane Austen, Charlotte Brontë, and Edith Wharton, respectively, depict a societal structure among the upper classes in which the formation of loyal and supportive friendships between women is virtually impossible. At worst, women are cruel and manipulative competitors for men; at best, they are ineffectual companions. Yet there is somewhat of a progression among these three novels that I believe is a reflection of the nearly 100 years that separates the first from the last.

In Austen's novel, women have virtually no power. One man, Mr. Darcy, is the catalyst for most of the events that lead to the happy conclusion of Austen's novel. There is rarely an instance in the novel when a woman truly helps another woman, and, in fact, it is more often the case that women intentionally thwart the designs of other women. Jane Eyre, the title character of Brontë's book, differs from the women in Austen's in that she has a considerable amount of inner strength. However, that strength seems to derive from some divine or natural power. And her strength is not an end of happiness in itself. Rather, it is her means to achieving a marriage with Rochester, and that marriage is equated with happiness for Jane. Whatever power it is that enables Jane to attain happiness, the support of female companions is never the major factor in guiding her through her troubles.

Lily Bart, the major character in *The House of Mirth,* attempts to assert her independence from men. Unlike Jane Eyre, Lily is not a woman of extraordinary inner strength. In addition, she is the product of a society that breeds women to be wives and thus does not prepare them to survive—let alone to be happy—on their own. But the atmosphere of change that existed in the United States during the time that Wharton's novel is set enabled her protagonist to believe—or perhaps better, to be fooled into believing—that she could survive on her own. Lily is wrong. What Lily misses—and what Wharton clearly saw—is that she does not have to do it on her own. She can lean on other women—two of whom offer their help. But Lily does not know how to do so. Nevertheless, Wharton was offering her readers a ray of hope—and a window onto what she hoped would be the future. Wharton believed that women's bonds with one another would be the means to their empowerment.

Mary Gordon wrote that "We have little romance or lore of female friendship in our culture."[7] Thus, it is not surprising that many believe, often without evidence, that women are untrustworthy and disloyal friends. This belief is in our collective unconscious. However, it is important to note that many contemporary female novelists write of female friendship very differently from the way earlier writers did. Mary Gordon, in *Final Payments,* and Gloria Naylor, in *The Women of Brewster Place,* elevate loyalty between women friends to a moral level. In an essay titled "Female Friendship in the Contemporary *Bildungsroman*," Payant discusses Joan Chase, Ella Leffland, and Alice Walker:

> Whereas in the past women were often portrayed in the culture as rivals, usually for the affections of a man, today we see themes emphasizing the gifts women give each other. One of the most exciting developments in contemporary literature by women has been this exploration of the bonds of enduring female friendship, especially its central importance in the development of a young protagonist. Such books have given thousands of women new insights into their experiences, as they ponder their own youths and come to realize how much they owe their friends.[8]

Although there are far too many examples in contemporary fiction of women's importance to one another for all to be included here, the voice of Toni Morrison must not be excluded. Morrison wrote of her title character in *Sula:*

> Nel was the one person who had wanted nothing from her, who had accepted all aspects of her ... Nel was the first person who had been real to her, whose name she knew, who had seen as she had the slant of life that made it possible to stretch it to its limits. . . .[9]

In the final words of the book we feel Nel's agony as she only now understands how she has felt about Sula upon the latter's death:

> [T]he loss pressed down on her chest and came up into her throat. "We was girls together," she said as though explaining something. "Oh Lord, Sula," she cried, "Girl, girl, girlgirlgirl!"
>
> It was a fine cry—loud and long—but it had no bottom and it had no top, just circles and circles of sorrow.[10]

The novels discussed here point to certain cultural attitudes that have changed a great deal over the past hundred years and others that have remained remarkably similar. Certainly, the protagonists of Gordon's and Naylor's novels, among others, depend on their friends in ways Austen and Brontë may not have been able to conceive of. However, as we see in the agony of Morrison's Nel, the picture is complicated. In virtually all of the contemporary novels mentioned, the friendships bring pain as well as joy. Relationships with men often negatively impact the women's relationships with each other. The women often struggle to figure out how to have the friendship they yearn for within the context of a culture that, as Gordon and Woolf both pointed out, regards women as untrustworthy and disloyal and, therefore, women's friendships as at times unimportant and/or inferior to men's. It is important to understand the women's friendships in the current study within such a cultural context.

Woolf wrote that fiction overall was weakened by its failure to explore women's relationships with one another.[11] Certainly, the failure of formal research to address those same concerns casts significant doubt on traditionally accepted beliefs about women's lives. The fiction discussed here points to the importance of close female friendships to women and highlights the need for an exploration of those friendships among the lives of actual women. Without an understanding of what women mean to each other, we cannot understand women's lives.

MY RESEARCH METHODS

The method of in-depth interviewing I used to gather my data falls under the umbrella of *qualitative research*. Whereas quantitative researchers generally begin with one or more hypotheses they want to test using measurement tools, statistical analysis, and a large and varied sample of subjects, qualitative researchers endeavor to gather data by delving much deeper to gain an understanding of a smaller number of people. An aim of qualitative research is to develop what is called *grounded theory.* That is, the researcher develops theory as she begins to understand the data—as the pieces are gradually put together. Qualitative methods are founded on the idea that we can gain fresh understandings about people by listening closely to individuals and learning about their experiences. Many commonly accepted theories about human behavior and human thought were developed using research with men—usually white, heterosexual men. Ideas about "the norm" were deduced from such studies. Thus, those whose behaviors were unlike these men were considered to be abnormal and in need of some sort of help to move closer to the so-called norm. Qualitative researchers often seek to challenge such traditionally held beliefs, particularly about those marginalized—like women—in some way by society. Thus, qualitative methodologies are often considered to be feminist in nature because they afford new, nontraditional perspectives on people's lives.

I set three criteria before I began to recruit volunteers for my study. Each of the seven participants had one or two female friends they considered to be a best friend and each considered herself to be heterosexual. Although I was not altogether comfortable with eliminating out-of-hand all those women who identify themselves as lesbian, bisexual, or some other sexual orientation, after talking with some lesbian and bisexual women, I came to believe that, on a sexual level, there might be fundamental differences between best friendships involving lesbian and bisexual women and those involving heterosexual women. This anecdotal evidence was confirmed by a book I later read titled *Lesbian Friendships: For Ourselves and Each Other.*[12] The essays contained in that book confirmed for me that for many lesbian women, the taboo most heterosexual women face against becoming sexually involved with their female friends is removed. Because I wanted to explore sexual aspects or feelings, I decided it best in this study to focus solely on women who identify themselves as heterosexual.

All but one woman met the third criterion: the women were to be twenty-four or older. I decided to include a slightly younger woman after talking with her about her interest in participating. The oldest woman was fifty-four at the start of the study. On a questionnaire, five indicated that they were European American, one Asian American, and one African American. Six of the women considered themselves to be of middle socioeconomic status and one said she was of upper-middle socioeconomic status. All of the women had a graduate degree and/or were in graduate school. Three of the women were married and two were engaged. Two of the married women had adult children. None of the others had children.

I conducted two in-depth interviews with each of the participants over a year's span. The first and second interviews ranged from three to six months apart. To begin the first interview, I asked open-ended and general questions such as "Please tell me the story of your friendship." I wanted the women to tell me about their experiences without much guidance from me. Thus, although I directed the course of the interviews, I tried wherever possible to follow each participant's lead. I believe this methodological approach affords a depth of understanding that many other approaches cannot attain. In allowing the data to guide me during the interviews and throughout the research process, I endeavored to remain as open as possible to the new ideas my participants presented me with.

After all the interviews and much of the analysis was completed, I sent six of the seven participants narratives written in each of their respective voices. (I could not contact the seventh person, but still included her in the study.) I asked them to give me their honest reactions. All of the women felt that I had accurately reflected their experiences and feelings.

After I had transcribed the audiotaped interviews, I analyzed the data. Qualitative analysis is a painstaking process. I began by writing codes for virtually every line of text on the hard copy of the interviews and continued revising the codes during the many months of analysis. Coding enables (some might say, forces) the researcher to apply meaning to the participants' words. Some codes I used were *best friend versus husband, hurt feelings,* and *conflict.* I then placed the many codes into fewer larger categories.

Throughout the coding process, and after it, I wrote many memos to myself, trying to make sense of the vast amounts of data I had. I experimented with many ways of organizing the codes into larger categories. I was constantly struggling to make new meanings of them. One of the things I did to help myself out was to write portions of the data as poems, as Patai describes doing. Patai uses this method for presenting her participants' words, because "[t]here is . . . a distance separating the spoken word from the written word that is insurmountable."[13] The poems allow participants' rhythms of speech to emerge. Thus, I would take a particular passage that was troubling me and find the place that it occurred on the tape. I would then replay it with the transcript in front of me. At each pause, I would put a slash on the hard copy. At times I would have to replay a sentence several times to get the rhythm just right. I then would type out the poem, starting a new line after each slash. Reading my participants' words in this form opened up the text in ways I could not have imagined when I was trying to understand it in prose form. I forced myself to try to code each line of the poem. Through that effort, new meanings invariably emerged. (See Appendix A for an example of a passage before and after it is written in poem-form.)

Over time, I began to link the categories together to see patterns among the participants. Eventually, the themes *competition between women, neediness and dependency,* and *knowing and understanding* emerged to link the individual stories together. These themes, combined with the particulars of each woman's experience, helped me to see beyond stereotypical constructions. Although these relationships are a wonderful and vital part of so many women's lives, they are accompanied by some real difficulties. In other words, there is far more to them than the competitiveness of Betty and Veronica's friendship in the *Archie* comics or the unconditional self-sacrifice of Thelma and Louise's, from the movie of the same name.

HOW THE FINDINGS ARE PRESENTED

My findings are presented in two ways: first-person stories and discussions of themes. The stories reflect the voices of the participants, but are written by me. Paul Atkinson writes of a "tension between the readability of the written text and the complexity of the original phenomenon. . . ."[14] That is, the more comprehensible the writer renders the spoken word, the less true to the actual words she or he will be. In writing the stories, in particular, I felt acutely the tension that Atkinson describes. However, although I altered some words and added transitions to make the stories more fluid, I took great pains to maintain the unique voices and to allow each personality to emerge. As I shaped the women's stories, I tried to enter into their narratives and hear the women speak from an intimate perspective. It is important to remember, however, that in both forms of presentation, I have constructed meaning from the women's words.

I chose to present my findings in these two narrative forms because each allows for a different understanding of the data. The stories enable the reader to view each woman's experiences more holistically. They give a comprehensive perspective with which to understand the women's words, providing background, history, and motivations. Although my voice is heard from time to time, the reader has a greater opportunity with these narratives to form his or her own ideas and opinions and to react intellectually and emotionally to the stories they are reading. At the end of each one, I discuss one or more aspects of the story that made a particular impression on me.

In contrast, the thematic discussions, while providing a less comprehensive view of the individual stories, allow a far greater depth of analysis so that patterns and similarities among the stories emerge. It becomes clear how the women's experiences relate to one another. In these chapters, the reader is able to consider the experiences in the context of the other stories, as well as in the context of related theory.

Clearly, these two narrative forms complement each other. Where one examines the specifics of each story, the other allows for in-depth analysis. While one allows the reader to develop impressions as he or she hears the women's voices, the other provides the reader with a guide to understanding the women's experiences in a more theoretical manner. Either of these two forms alone would be insufficient for presenting my findings, but together they reveal the richness of the data. I alternate between the forms in my presentation for the sake of readability. If readers were presented with all seven stories in a row, the impact of the last story would surely be far less than the impact of the first.

WHAT THIS BOOK IS NOT

While I am secure in the knowledge that my methodology afforded me a flexibility and insight that could not have been gained from a more quantitative model, I believe it important to note what this study and my conclusions cannot be. My interviewees are, by my own choosing, heterosexual. They all have high levels of education, are middle class, and are American. All but two are white. Of course, even if I had somehow managed to obtain a participant group that contained women from seven different ethnic, racial, socioeconomic, and sexual categories, my findings would be no more valid or credible. It is not my aim to prove certain hypotheses about women's friendships or to compare, for example, how white and black women structure their respective relationships. It is certainly not my intent to speak for all women and their closest friendships. Rather, I provide a snapshot of female best friendship, and thus, of women's lives. The themes that emerged for these seven women may not have relevance in each and every woman's best friendship, but I believe they have value in helping us to understand women's lives and relationships, in general.

Chapter 2

Linda

Linda was a fifty-year-old married white woman with two grown children, studying for her doctorate. As I drove to her house, I was looking forward to the first interview, because our earlier encounters had left me with a very positive impression of her. When I arrived for both interviews, she offered me a cup of coffee from the pot she had just brewed. At one point during the first interview, during a break, Linda gave me a tour of her house. We conducted both interviews at her kitchen table.

THE STORY

Linda has two best friends—Emily and Carol. She begins her narrative by telling me how her friendship with Emily, whom she met first, began. A theme that reverberates throughout their relationship emerges early both in Linda's rendering of the story and in the chronology of the friendship. That is, Linda perceives that the relationship has often largely been on Emily's terms. Indeed, that is how the friendship begins:

Emily

I met Emily probably twenty-two years ago, when I moved into the town she lived in. I had a baby. She lived two doors down and was pregnant. She was a friend of a friend. So one day I just rang the bell and said hello, and we kind of chatted. But Emily didn't really feel like she had a connection to me. So at the beginning, we were just kind of formal. And it really wasn't pursued. She didn't really respond. And I guess I was just looking for friends. I wasn't from the area. We came here for my husband's job. So I think I pursued it at the beginning, but she was just kind of nice. She's very nice, so she didn't say yes or no, one way or the other. But she gave birth a couple months later, and then we became very close because she would ask me all kinds of questions about being a mother. I think that gave her a reason to be friends.

She's very, very close with her older sister and I am the oldest girl in my family. I think that's a comfortable role for me. I think I kind of became an older sister to her. So I was always the one that gave advice. And I did have all this experience with children, because I came from a family of seven. So I was very comfortable with babies. I think she looked to me as a kind of a mentor/mother. And as a big sister. I'm several years older than her.

We lived together there for another, I think, year and a half, two years. We were neighbors for those two years. And we were very close friends when the kids were young. We would have play groups together and we'd see each other two or three times a week. We'd go shopping together and on walks, pushing the kids in the strollers. And then she bought a home in a nearby town. And we bought a home here. And we stayed friends. Once the kids got into school, we saw each other once a week or once every two weeks. And even though the times have gotten farther, now, twenty years later—with both of us working, we see each other maybe once every two months—we just pick up where we left off. It's just been an ongoing friendship.

Yet, Linda has not been entirely passive in the relationship. When something has been important enough to her, she has found a way to exert her wishes:

Early on in the friendship we would double date. The four of us would go out. But as the years went by, it became more of a female friendship. We would go out in the evenings during the week when the kids were young, because our husbands would be home. So she and I would go out for dinner, rather than going out with our husbands on a Saturday night. It became less of a family friendship and more of an individual friendship between her and me. I think that's something that I kind of chose to do, and I don't know if she just went along with it. I enjoyed being with her alone more than I enjoyed being with her in couples. It gave us more time to talk and to be intimate . . . to talk about our husbands, or talk about our kids in a way you wouldn't talk about them in front of your husband. I think I wanted the friendship just between us.

Linda takes me through the process of their deepening relationship—the ups and downs, the starts and stops:

I remember the friendship got intimate fairly quickly, because she's kind of a very honest person. One day she called me up and she said, "I can't believe it. I just hit Jon and I think I really hurt him. I feel terrible. Come over right away." I mean I would never call up someone and say, "I hit my kid and hurt him." But she was very open, so the intimacy started right away. I mean to me, after just being friends for maybe nine or ten months, she would say things that seemed very personal. It wasn't like there was any time span between meeting her and then becoming really good friends with her. I think I respond to other people being open first. I tend to be more closed. And if others don't want to be open, I won't expose myself, nor would I ask them a personal question.

I always thought she had this perfect marriage. But about ten or twelve years into the friendship, she became sick. She was nauseous and depressed, and I didn't know why. She's a very happy person, not depressed at all. I found out years later that she had been having trouble for quite some time with her husband, and she was really kind of falling apart. But that she didn't share with me. And I was really surprised when I found out, considering we were so close, that she didn't tell me at the time what was going on. We would complain about our husbands, bitch about this and bitch about that, but she never really let on that there was anything major. But I didn't spend a lot of time analyzing why she hadn't told me.

I had always talked to her about my marriage, so I was surprised that she didn't share . . . back, if that's the word. I mean I can analyze it now. She always had kind of this picture-perfect marriage and these three lovely children, and from the outside everything looked wonderful, as in any life. But I guess I felt hurt and a little left out. And I felt bad for her that she was having a hard time and she didn't share it. I didn't understand it. Was it so painful that she couldn't share it? Was she embarrassed? Or she didn't want to say that she didn't have this wonderful life? I guess I didn't take it personally that she didn't share it with me. I took it more as seeing a part of her that I didn't see before. I guess I felt she had this need to keep up this façade for me. And that didn't really hurt me as much as it bothered me that she needed to do that. But I never asked her. I never said, "Gee, why didn't you tell me you were having trouble?"

One reason I figured was that she always confided in her older sister. And maybe you just need one person to talk to. And that was the person that she talked to. So she didn't really need to share with me. But it was really only in that one instance, I think. She always used to call me up and say, "I wouldn't tell anyone but Nan." Nan's her sister. "You're the only one besides Nan." And I like Nan. Occasionally we would go out as a threesome. I never felt in competition with her, because I knew Em was very close to her . . . and I think Em viewed me kind of like a sister.

Although Linda at first says she has not spent a lot of time analyzing why Emily did not tell her about her marital difficulties, she clearly has put a lot of thought into it. Also, it seemed to me that she did feel hurt, despite her protestations to the contrary. (As Linda's narrative continues, it will become more evident why she would be loath to acknowledge feelings of hurt within her friendships.) Linda also may have felt some confusion and discomfort with the realization that the relationship was not exactly what she thought it had been. Emily had not been sharing at the level and with the honesty that Linda believed she was, or that Linda, herself, had been. The history of the friendship had to be subtly rewritten.

But ultimately, reality comes to match Linda's expectations and beliefs about the relationship:

But when she did share that years later, the friendship deepened. After that, we did share everything. We talked about everything. And then it was like flat out, "This is it; this is my life," warts and everything, for both of us. And maybe more so for her than for me, because I didn't have a need to keep a façade up. I had a need to talk about my problems, whereas she had more of a need to keep the façade, because she could talk to someone else. But once her façade was down, we could talk about anything. It really kind of grounded us in honesty. I think she knows everything there is to know about me.

As Linda continues her narrative, she provides more insight into Emily and the dynamics of the friendship:

One of the reasons I thought they had an ideal marriage was that it seemed like she could have anything she wanted. Because that's what I saw. But I didn't realize until she told me about this trouble, that her husband was very self-centered. Things had to be his way. That surprised me, because if anything, I thought Em was a little self-centered. Things had to be her way. Because in our friendship she got what she wanted. When it involved the two of us, she always chose what we did for the day, where we went, how we did it, and she'll say to me, "Oh is that OK?" And I'd say, "Yeah, it's fine." I mean I really don't care. And if I said to her one day, "No, I want to go to this restaurant," I'm sure she'd say, "Fine, let's go." But the next time if I said, "I want to try this restaurant," I don't know how she'd feel. I don't know how long we'd be friends if I was always the one saying, "Let's do this; let's do this."

Thus, not only does Linda see this aspect of the relationship as being on Emily's terms, she wonders if the friendship could sustain Linda's taking more control. However, because of the realities of their current relationship, she does not have to dwell on her concerns:

I think maybe what helps our relationship, and she's said this also, is that it's not a day-to-day thing. Because that puts a lot of stress on a friendship. Our kids never competed, because we lived in different communities. She has a friend that lives across the street from her who she's very good friends with. This woman really adores Em, but she has a girl the same age as Em's daughter and that causes trouble. So in a way our distance has enabled us not to deal with a lot of day-to-day things. And I think that helps a friendship a lot. It keeps it very ideal, I think. You know, it's almost like not living together with a guy or living together and not being married. There are fewer demands and therefore the relationship is easier. And I think for Em, our friendship doesn't involve the balancing act some of her other friendships have. It works very well for her.

Actually, that whole thing about her having her own way isn't really an issue anymore, because we don't see each other that often. But I think if it went back to being a day-to-day kind of relationship that might have to change. Because I'd have to say, "Well, look, I don't want to do what you want to do all the time," and that might upset the balance of how you view the friendship . . . the needs that we both get from each other. So if her need for me is to always go along with what she wants to do, and I'm not fulfilling that need, then she won't look to me as much for friendship. But that's an old issue. I don't think either of us would want a day-to-day friendship anymore. I don't want to say that kind of friendship is childish, but I feel like I don't need to talk to someone every day.

Yet Linda does recognize that the fact that she and Emily have not had overt conflicts is likely due primarily to Linda's desire to avoid confrontation:

> Em and I don't fight at all. I don't know if that's good or bad. I don't think I do well with fights. I think that's probably a lot of conflict avoidance on my part. And I think it does lead to some distance, even though it's a best friendship. I think I'm uncomfortable asserting myself. And so it's easier not to have to do that. So maybe my inability to deal with the problems keeps the friendship at a distance, where it's safe and comfortable for me, in that one aspect.
>
> Sometimes, though, I would get annoyed about things, like we would make a date and she'd cancel it. And I would be very careful to save this date and work my life around this, and then she'll call up the day before and say, "Oh, I have to cancel." Which I've learned that she does, so then I've just said, "OK this is part of who she is" and now when we make a date, if something better comes up for me, I'll cancel too. I think that used to annoy me more, because I would never cancel on her. But now I have canceled a few times. But we don't see each other as often, so when we make a date we really try and keep it. But she's still more ready to cancel it than I would be.

Again, we see Emily as exerting more control over aspects of the friendship. But as Linda goes on, her role in this dynamic becomes more evident:

> And I've thought about this, too. . . . I think part of the friendship comes from Em. I don't know if it's because I don't want to be needy. Whether it's a kind of independence or a kind of boxing off on my part. So I'm not going to be the one to call you. I kind of wait for people to call me. And months will go by and I won't call, because I don't have the need to call . . . and she'll call and say, "Where are you? I haven't heard from you." And maybe it's partly because I don't want to be perceived as needy. So even though I might want to call her, I don't.

Linda finishes her story about her friendship with Emily with some insights into her friend's character:

> Em and I are a lot alike. She doesn't dwell on the negatives, and she's an optimist. And I'm an optimist too. I don't dwell on negatives. If something's not right, you talk about it and you try and fix it, you don't just dwell on it. If it can be fixed, fix it. And if it can't be fixed, you learn to live with it and you make the best of it, which is her attitude also.
>
> And she was always a good mother. I think that was very important to me. I've seen that with my friends that I've stayed friends with, or even with people I'm not that good friends with but whom I admire. I think one quality that's important to me is that they be a good mother. And Em was. We had lots of similar ideas about mothering, and I think that kind of solidified the friendship. Kids were important to us; to be a good mother was important. The kids came first.

And Em's a very kind person. She would never say anything to hurt anyone's feelings. Neither would I. My mother-in-law has a saying about a friend: a friend is someone who'll never hurt your feelings. I think that's true to a large extent. Because I've had other friendships, that at the time were very intimate in a talking sort of way. But they have said something that hurts my feelings, and I know that becomes the end of the friendship. Em's never done that, nor have I. I don't ever do that to anyone, I don't think. I mean I don't ever say anything that's mean or to hurt someone's feelings.

But I guess if Em ever said anything hurtful, I probably would let it go. But I can't imagine her doing that. A friend just wouldn't. And she's said things that weren't hurtful, but were insightful that, at first, I felt like, "Oh, well who are you to say that type of thing?" But then after I think about it, I realize it was really insightful and it was really interesting. And it wasn't said to hurt, certainly. And I didn't take it that way. But when other people say things, I just let it roll of my back. Em has said and done things that have annoyed me, but I just let it go.

With some people I've heard about and from what I've seen with some of her other friends, there's competition. Em and I never really competed, because we didn't go in the same social circle. I don't have a big social circle because my husband and I aren't big socialites. But she is, and she had a very large group of friends. And I think she enjoyed that for what it was worth, but I think she saw my friendship as a refuge from that. A place where she didn't need to compete, she didn't have to talk about her last trip to the Bahamas and where she's going Christmas, because that's not important to me. If I was going away, I would share it with her because I would be excited about going away, not so I could name drop the latest vacation places. And I think that helped the friendship—that we didn't compete. But that's one way that she's a little different than I am.

Em's a physical therapist. She got married right out of school, so she was very young when she got married. And, another thing is that she gives off an aura of being ditzy and spacey, but she's very perceptive and very smart. My mother-in-law said to me that she used to wonder how I could be friends with Em because she thought she was a kind of a space head. But I just always knew she was bright. My husband once in a while would also say something negative about her intelligence, and I'd say, "No, you don't understand. She's a very intelligent person." She just is not book-smart, because that was not stressed in her family. It was stressed that she get married young and make a good marriage. That was what was important for her to do and be. But in spite of that, she's a very intelligent person.

She decided to go back to school, but she was very nervous about feeling stupid. I told her not to worry about it, that everybody feels that way at first. And once she got back into it, all of that changed. Her self-image changed. All of a sudden she could be intellectual and be very analytical. And I think that changed the way we talked together. I think maybe she always felt a little insecure with me about her intelligence. I mean I'm just saying this because I was always book smart and because I had a master's. School was always very important to my husband and me, and to my kids. We always stressed school. Whereas her husband didn't finish college. Academics wasn't really stressed in her house. But once she went back to school, which was about ten years ago, that kind of changed, and that really deepened our conversations. I think she felt much more comfortable talking intellectually about things, about books, with me.

Carol

As Linda begins her story of her friendship with Carol, we see some parallels to her friendship with Emily, which brings up interesting questions about how women in general form friendships and what we look for in those relationships at different times in our lives:

Carol lives next door, so I met her when I moved in here. She came over to welcome me. She brought some cookies and said that if I ever needed anything I should call her. She has two boys. Her younger son was the same age as my son, so the boys would play. We were just neighborly friends. She would borrow a cup of sugar. And we would do things back and forth with the kids. But it wasn't until about eight years ago, when I started my whole career thing, that we became friendlier. It became more of a friendship, more of an intimate talking-type thing. I talk to her about once a week; we call each other on the phone. And occasionally we'll go to a movie.

I became more friendly with her, as I said, after the kids got older. We would go into the City and go to museums. She's a poet, so we would talk a lot about poetry. We'd analyze it from our different perspectives. And she's a big reader. But she's terribly insecure about being smart. She has a husband who didn't make her feel good about herself. He wouldn't say, "You're great," or anything. The world kind of revolved around him. She would cater to him. He was very critical. So as a result, she always felt very insecure about her intelligence, about doing anything right. I kind of saw my role as to build her self-esteem up and tell her, "Look, your poetry is wonderful."

I think we also became close when I was having trouble in my marriage and I was more willing to talk about it with her. And then she opened up to me. I think that made us closer friends. I think that makes you more human to one another. It just shows that everyone has problems and you have to deal with them. And it made me feel closer, I guess, to share my problems with her and have her share hers with me. And it isn't always sharing problems; it's sharing your life more than sharing your problems. It's just talking about the good things and the bad things with your kids. And it's also that when I share, she can share. It's not like, "Oh, well my kid would never do that"-type of thing. There's not a criticism and there's not a gulf. If she never talked about her concerns with her kids, I'd think, "Oh, well she thinks her kids are great, so I'm not going to talk about my concerns with my kids anymore because I don't want her to think my kids aren't as good as her kids." But it's not like that.

And when our kids left for college and we both had a profession, we talked a lot about how we view ourselves as professionals. Like sometimes she wouldn't be home in time to cook dinner, and her husband really expected a traditional wife, whereas mine didn't. So we would talk those things through. What are your obligations if your husband is supporting you? What are your obligations as a wife? I guess we explored our lives within the context of each other and how we viewed responsibilities and roles and professions.

At the start of both friendships, Emily and Carol were neighbors of Linda. Both friendships truly began when areas of commonality were reached that were most significant to the women at their particular stage of life. Linda and Emily's friendship took off when they both had young children. For Linda and Carol, the friendship did not begin to get intimate until Linda's focus shifted somewhat away from her family and toward her professional studies. In addition, Linda sees both friendships as having begun when the women began to share feelings about their marriages. She also describes her friends as having been less secure than she of their intellectual abilities. In both cases, she tries to bolster her friends' confidence.

Linda goes on to talk about what Carol is like:

> Carol's very nice. She's very creative. She's a couple of years older than I am. And she's a good mother. Mothering came first. She also didn't work. Neither did Emily. We were all stay-home moms. She's an attractive woman, and easy to talk to. And she's a lot of fun. I enjoy being with her. She's easy to talk to, but she's more opinionated than Em, or she'll give you her opinion more. But I value it. I mean, she's never said anything that I would disagree with. So maybe we have the same viewpoint. But, you know, if we talk about mothers-in-law or sisters and brothers or in-laws generally—we talk a lot about in-laws—she'll say something about my situation, not giving advice, just in telling the way she's seeing it. Which is interesting. She's usually pretty perceptive. And I don't tend to do that unless she asks me. I value her insights and opinion, so that isn't a problem. Actually it's a strength. Sometimes you need that distance. When you're having a problem and you talk about it, and someone else'll say, "Oh, but this is the way it is or this is the way I see it," it kind of helps you see things in a different way. Carol does that much more than Em would. Em wouldn't give an opinion unless she knows I want it, where Carol gives an opinion much more readily. But obviously it doesn't offend me, because I'm still friends with her.

Perhaps because Linda and Carol are neighbors, their husbands seem to be more of a presence in their friendship than is the case with Linda and Emily's:

> I don't really like Stuart, her husband. He's very arrogant. He doesn't treat her nicely. I don't like him because of that. I mean, a lot of men can be arrogant, and that doesn't mean I wouldn't necessarily like them, but he's very, very demeaning to Carol—although it's changed some in the past four or five years. But when I'm with him, you wouldn't know I don't like him. We can talk and everything. But I don't really like him. Of course, I would never say that to her. But she can say negative things about him to me. She'll tell me what he did to her, but I don't ever comment. My husband doesn't like him either.
> My husband feels closer to Em than to Carol. Sometimes when Carol has some things on her mind, and when she gets on a topic, she just starts talking and talking and talking, and she realizes it at the end, and she says, "Oh, I've been doing all the talking. How are you?" So sometimes she doesn't really listen. But it's not an issue for me, and I have never said anything to her about it. And

she does turn around and say, "Oh, I've been doing all this talking. Let's talk about you." So it's not as if she talks and I listen all the time. It's just that when she talks she *doesn't* listen.

Carol and Emily

Linda sheds more light on her best friends and friendships as she compares them and her feelings about them. She also sheds light on herself:

I'm actually . . . I was going to say better friends with Em than with Carol. But I think it's just the friendships are a little different. The honesty is still there and the sharing is still there. I mean if I had to say which one I liked more, I'd say I liked Em more than Carol, but I still consider Carol a best friend. And I think she does me also. But Carol tends to be a little more quiet. And Em's more bubbly. And I probably share a little more with Em than with Carol, but it's only that it's a little deeper. I think I've shared everything with Carol, too. I don't have any secrets, whatever that means. But maybe I feel a little more comfortable sharing with Em, because she's not as critical as I see Carol. Carol can be a little opinionated. So I might say something to Em that I wouldn't say to Carol, because I wouldn't want Carol to be critical of me. Whereas Em I know won't be.

It's interesting, though, sometimes I think about where I fit into their group of friends. I know they both consider me a best friend, but I think about how I fit in aspect-wise, not competition-wise. When I look at Carol and I look at her friends, I notice a lot of them are much wealthier than she is, and she's comfortable with that. And yet when I look at Em, I don't think she would be, because from what I observe, she's always the most well-off of all her friends. So I've wondered where I fit into their social structures, in terms of how they view me, more than how I view them. Because in a way, we're all kind of financially the same, Carol and I and Em. So it's interesting for me to see who their other friends are. I'm not competitive and show-offish, so they're not with me. And Carol is not, but her husband is. It's always a bone of contention with her that he has all these friends in the country club. She says, "I'm happy to stay in my house and to read my book on the weekend, and he wants to go out and do all these things." And I'm actually more like him in that way—and Em. I would be into doing the country club thing if my husband were. So it's just a difference in Carol's and my personality that maybe enables us to be friends. She always says she'd rather be with arty people who wouldn't think showing off their new Rolex is the first priority.

So with her and me it's not an issue at all, what I'm wearing or anything. But with Em, I don't know. She's not show-offish, and she's very kind and very genuine, but when you look at her you don't get that impression. She has everything. Only she's not super wealthy. She's well-off and very comfortable, and her husband's in business, so they have a very nice lifestyle. And she has a new car every year, and has the latest piece of jewelry, and she likes it. I don't really know if she does it to show off and be better than anyone. She just really likes to have those things. And as I said, all of her friends are of similar circumstance. No one is really wealthier than she is, which I just find interesting. Which is different than Carol. Carol and Stuart have a lot of friends that are a lot wealthier than they are.

But competition's not an issue in either of those friendships, maybe because I don't make it an issue. I'm very happy when good things happen to them.

Both Em and Carol are more ready to express how they feel about me and about how much they value our friendship than I am to tell them. For a time, I was thinking of moving, and they both said, "Oh, if you go away, we'll still make it a point to get together." They expressed apprehension or dismay that I would move away. But I don't think I've ever expressed those feelings back to either of them. I think they're more outgoing than I am in that way. I take my cues from them. I guess I'm more withholding than they are. I don't say things like that spontaneously. Whereas they do.

I guess I think of my friendships as best friendships because we would do anything for each other. That's what a best friend does. If you called them up and said, "I need a favor," they would do it. Even if it meant taking a day off from work. You know, "I just need you. You have to come over today." I think both she and Carol would do that. As I would do for them. I think I would assume that they would be here for me, whatever that means. But they don't have to be there for me, because I'm not demanding. I'm very independent. I've never asked them to do that. I'm not the type to say, "Oh, I'm falling apart, you have to come over." And the same with them. Maybe we're all the same type. We're not needy people. But if either of them asked, or if I asked, we would be there for the other.

And I also think that they know me. And I know them. And that, number one, it's comfortable, number two, you don't have to play any games. You don't have to act anything other than who you are because you know they like you for who you are. And, three, it saves a lot of time. We always kid about, if I say something to Em—more so than to Carol—we always joke around that we don't have to give a long explanation of what we mean, because we both know. And so that's easy. For example, with some past situation with my son, they know how I felt about it. So if I'm talking about something now, I don't have to offer long explanations because everything's already been discussed and understood.

I also think basically we're the same people. I guess this is important with friends—and maybe that's why I don't have a hundred friends—but your values have to be the same. I don't know if I could be friends with someone who was, oh I don't know, who was real snobby or who was real racist. Because I just wouldn't like that person. And so I think that the things that I value are the things that they value, and that we react to things the same way. I mean we don't always react to things the same, but in general, we kind of view things the same. I don't know if I could be friends with someone who was really different in that way.

FURTHER REFLECTIONS:
KEEPING SOME DISTANCE

One of the aspects of Linda's story that has struck me from the beginning is the degree to which she seems to be guarded in her friendships with Emily and Carol. She says that in relationships, in general, she is not one to take the lead in being very open. Instead, if others open up first, she then may respond in kind. If they do not do so, she will neither expose herself nor ask personal questions of them. Although at this time, Linda does not seem to be guarded with her two best friends on that level—that is, she says that she and her friends are quite open with each other and there are no longer any secrets—she finds it virtually impossible to tell either Emily or Carol how she feels, good or bad, about them. She guards those emotions very closely.

One of the most poignant times this subject comes up is when Linda tells me that in their friendship, Emily has tended to decide what they do together. She explains that this was particularly true in the past, when they saw each other regularly. For example, Emily would have some idea for a place to go for lunch and Linda would agree. Linda wonders, however, what would happen to the friendship if she started to be the one to suggest places to go and to assert her desires more often. She realizes that if the relationship went back to one in which they had far more frequent contact, she would find it difficult to return to a dynamic in which it felt to her as if Emily always "got what she wanted." But she speculates that if she were to be honest with Emily about how she felt, the friendship might not survive in its current form. She feels that her assertion might upset the balance of the relationship. Further, it occurs to her that if their friendship is one in which each fulfills the needs of the other, she would no longer be fulfilling Emily's need for Linda "to always go along with what she wants to do." Emily might then choose to look elsewhere for friendship—to a place where that need could be fulfilled.

Because Linda and Emily no longer have a day-to-day friendship, Linda feels that her concerns do not need to be addressed. However, it is not clear if Linda feels that way because it does not happen anymore or because she can accept it since she no longer sees Emily on a daily basis. Nevertheless, it seems likely that if the frequency of their contacts were to increase, Linda would find a way to deal with her feelings that did not involve revealing them to Emily.

Linda also says that she used to get annoyed at Emily when Emily would cancel dates. Although Linda does not express it to me, it is my sense that she felt hurt by Emily's actions. While Linda considered their dates to be special and important, Emily seemed to place less significance on them. Whatever Linda's feelings—annoyance, anger, hurt—she apparently had to do something with them. What she chose was to do to Emily what Emily was doing to her: She started to cancel if something else came up. This is not to say that Linda was playing a game in which she was showing Emily that she could be as cavalier about their friendship as Emily was apparently being. Rather, I think that Linda decided that she would not be as vulnerable to hurt—or annoyance—if she placed less significance in her own mind on those dates and left open the possibility that she could cancel if something better came along.

In both of these examples, Linda chooses to keep her feelings to herself and deal with them on her own, rather than talk about them with Emily. By doing so, she realizes that she is maintaining a distance in their friendship. She knows that she is uncomfortable with conflict and recognizes that by not asserting herself she is not dealing with the problems in the friendship. Yet, while she sees that her actions create distance, she also feels that the friendship is consequently at a place "where it's safe and comfortable for me."

However, Linda's avoidance of conflict has an additional element. Certainly, she is guarding against her own feelings of vulnerability, but it seems to me that she is also guarding against anything that could harm the friendship. She does so not only by searching for an outlet for her own anger and hurt that will not negatively impact the relationship, but also by not allowing for the possibility that friends sometimes do or say things that can be hurtful. When I ask her what she would do if Emily said something hurtful, she says that a friend would not hurt a friend. When Emily has said something to which she at first takes affront, she prefers to alter her perspective so that she can view it in a light that is not hurtful, rather than choose to feel hurt and either talk to Emily or live with the realization that her friend could be hurtful: "But then after I think about it, I realize it was really insightful and it was really interesting." In fact, Linda tells me a story about a friendship she once had that ended because Linda extricated herself from it after her friend said something hurtful.

Another example of Linda's avoidance of conflict is her attitude about competition. (See Chapter 5 for an in-depth discussion of competitive feelings.) Linda feels strongly that competition has no place in a friendship. She says that she is not at all competitive and that in this respect, her two friends follow her cue. They may be competitive in other relationships, but Linda believes she successfully prevents competitive feelings from entering their friendships with her. Furthermore, Linda tells me that she is wary of becoming friends with someone on a professional level because of the competitiveness that can develop. She says that although she has friends at school, she does not feel that she could maintain a friendship in which she thought the other person was becoming competitive.

Thus, Linda's guardedness has two levels. First, as a guarded person in general, she is wary of feeling vulnerable. Not only does she avoid discussing her anger with her friends, but she also does not readily tell her friends how important they are to her. It is very difficult for her to express to them how she feels toward them—whether those feelings are good or bad. At the second level, Linda is guarding the friendship. Her friendships with Emily and Carol are extremely important to her. They offer a place she can go, apart from her family, and have a one-on-one intimate relationship. She can talk to her friends about things she can to talk to no one else about, including her husband. At the same time that she recognizes that there is a distance in these friendships because of the things that are not discussed, she seems to fear for the changes that would necessarily result if they were discussed. Thus, Linda chooses to maintain the friendships she so values as they are rather than risk their equilibrium by allowing negative feelings to intrude.

Chapter 3

Nancy

Nancy is a forty-year-old single white woman, living alone in an apartment in a suburban community. She is pursuing a doctorate. Both of our interviews took place in her living room. From the very beginning, I found her to be open and forthcoming. She jumped right in and started talking before I had even finished asking her my first question. As a result, this interview began almost midstream in comparison to my other interviews. I followed her lead for awhile, and then brought her back to where I felt the interview needed to go.

However, I did find it difficult to ask Nancy certain things. In fact, she brought up some topics that I wanted to follow up on but never did. I wondered why it seemed so hard to ask her more about those issues. At some point during my analysis, it occurred to me that my hesitancy to dig deeper may have come from cues that Nancy had given. She had told me that she does not open up easily and that it is hard to really get to know her. That was what I had sensed when we were together.

THE STORY

Nancy begins our interview by taking me through her thought processes in deciding who of her friends she is going to talk to me about. For some women, the answer to the question, "Who is (are) your best friend(s)?" is immediate and obvious. They know exactly who their one or two best friends are. For others, it is less clear-cut. Usually, these women have several close friendships and are uncomfortable with the idea of placing them in some hierarchy. Others think of the term "best friendship" as something left over from childhood. Then some, like Nancy, have not given much thought to who their best

friends are and need some time to consider how exactly to define a
best friend:

> Well, actually it was very funny, because I hadn't thought about who my best
> friends are until you came to our class, and I thought, "Who is my best friend?"
> Because I have many friends. And then I was thinking, maybe it's the people that
> I see the most, but I thought about that and they aren't actually my best friends.
> So then I began to think about what exactly "best friend" means. Last week, one
> of my so-called best friends was leaving a job where we used to work together. I
> was thinking of the gift that I gave her, and I think it showed a very clear connec-
> tion to her. When they were planning the goodbye party for her, they called me for
> help, even though I haven't worked there for five years. So even though I don't
> see Lisa as much as I would like, she would be one of my best friends.
>   And then, I thought about my other friends. Another friend of mine, Claudia,
> had a big birthday party recently. There was this formal thing for her; it was her
> fortieth birthday. I couldn't go because I got sick that day, and I thought about how
> awful I felt, because I was her only friend invited from her past. So it was some-
> thing that I thought about. When you first asked for participants, I was thinking,
> "Who's my best friend? I have lots of best friends." I could name them all through
> each period of my life, but I never thought, recently, about it. I've thought about
> people I'm friendly with, people I love to talk to, people I feel close to. But then
> when I thought about it, I thought, "OK, it's Claudia and Lisa who are my best
> friends."

As Nancy takes me through her thought processes in figuring out
who her best friends are, she starts from the outside in. She sees that
the two sets of party-throwers recognize her importance to Claudia
and Lisa. That awareness of how others view these friendships serves
as an initial guidepost for exploring what these two women mean to
her—and why she would call them best friends:

> I think it's because they probably know me the best. I've had serious fights
> with both of them, but we've worked them through. They're not like those friends
> that you do things with, and as long as it's fine, it's fine. They're important enough
> that even when something happens that would make you very mad, and make
> them very mad at me, there's a bond there that makes you want to clean that up.
> To maintain that relationship. Whereas with other people, if there's some falling
> out, it's fine to let it go. You can just move on.
>   And they are both people that I would like in my life when I'm ninety. Claudia
> says that all the time. That when she's ninety, she still wants to be doing dinner or
> lunch, or something. And the other piece I think is really important, when I think
> of my style, is that most of my friends will say that I'm not very open. I mean I'm
> open enough, and I'm friendly enough, but to know me well is hard. And I would
> say that they know me well, in spite of myself.

Claudia and Lisa are Nancy's best friends because they know her
the best. She may see other friends more often, but she has not opened

up to them as she has to these two women. This idea of wanting to be fully known seems to resonate for many women. It is not easy to open ourselves up, but when we do and we are accepted for who we are, there is an enormous sense of relief. (See Chapter 11 for an in-depth discussion of knowing in best friendship.)

Claudia

I began each initial interview by asking the women to tell me the story of one of their best friendships (if they had two). Nancy chose to begin with Claudia. I think there were two reasons for this choice. First, she met Claudia several years before she met Lisa so it made sense from a storytelling perspective. But I think on a less conscious level, she chose to begin with Claudia because it was an easier, more straightforward story to tell. It is not difficult to understand the value Nancy places on this friendship. In contrast, as will become evident later, Nancy's relationship with Lisa has some puzzling aspects to it.

Nancy briefly tells me how she and Claudia met, and then begins to relate some problems they had early in their relationship:

I met Claudia probably my second week of college. Claudia wasn't happy on the floor where she was. She felt like she had no one to hang out with. One day I just happened to be walking by, and she just started babbling to me and we became friends. And then there were some competitions. Although I don't know if there were competitions, I never actually perceived it that way. There were many things that occurred that could have ruined the friendship. But there was something in our friendship that made us work on it.

Like that year, there was a guy, David, who went out with another friend of ours first semester. And I thought he was a jerk. But he used to come into my room all the time. And basically because he was a nice-looking guy, my roommate would give him her homework every single night. But over time he chilled with that a little, and we laughed a lot and got to know him. But he also laughed a lot with Claudia.

Every fall and spring there were these dances, and Claudia was expecting that he would ask her. She told everybody that. But he asked me. And that was a big issue for me. Two of our friends said that I should go—and I did. But it was a big deal, because Claudia was hurt.

I don't remember how the conversation went between us, but I know she came in to see me. We lived across the hall from each other, and she was actually pretty nice about it. She got over being mad, and we talked about it.

I can think of many other times with many other people that I've said something didn't matter when it did, and so it wasn't talked about. But Claudia doesn't let that happen. I can remember times when I've told Claudia that something didn't matter and she said it did. She knew it did. She can tell and she'll push.

Sometimes Claudia will be too pushy. But nonetheless, it's allowed a deep friendship.

And then I guess there was a lot of competition and conflict going on with grades and stuff. Claudia didn't care much about grades. Or I didn't think she did. But there was this incident that led to us talking a whole lot about competition—primarily on her side. At least I wasn't so aware of it. We had taken this test in a class we were both in. And the professor announced that only two people had passed, and they happened to get a 92 and a 96. Claudia usually didn't care. She was the most popular person in my college. She was very outgoing, and kind of a very powerful presence, so a lot of people were very intimidated and taken aback by her. And she was very smart, but very flippant about grades. And what happened is the papers were handed back, and Claudia saw her 92. And then she came up to me and asked me what I got. And I could tell that—I knew she was thinking that I failed. And I had the 96. And that led to us talking about the competition stuff.

Clearly, what stands out for Nancy about the early years of her friendship with Claudia is that they had conflicts and that those conflicts were resolved. It seems probable that dealing openly with difficult relationship issues was a somewhat new experience for Nancy. Claudia has always been the motivating force in their friendship in confronting issues that have come up between them. Nancy would likely let most things sit and hope that they dissipate with time. She knows that it is Claudia's persistence in forcing her to open up that has led to their deep intimacy, and she very much appreciates this quality in her friend.

Nancy goes on to tell of a recent problem between them, revealing that this dynamic of difficulty and resolution motivated by Claudia continues today:

The most recent sort of conflict we had was about this party. I really meant to go. But I got very sick, and it was a two-and-a-half, three-hour drive to get to the party. I had to teach the next morning. And I had a splitting headache, a runny nose, a fever. I just couldn't do it. So I called that morning and apologized. Afterward, I kept e-mailing her, and I didn't get a response for like two weeks. So I could tell that she was mad. But finally when she got the gift I had sent her—it had been delivered to a neighbor's accidentally—she realized that I didn't just slap it together. It showed how much I cared. And then she e-mailed me.

But she was mad that I didn't go to the party, and on some level I thought she was being a baby about it. I understand it was her party, and yes it was a big deal, and yes I did want to come. But she can't always have her way. And I couldn't do it. I really wanted to do it, but I just couldn't. It's just that sometimes she can be a little egocentric. But on the other hand, on some level, I feel very good about it because it was that important to her that I come. I was the only person invited from her past. And it made me feel good that her friends got it that it was meaningful enough to invite me.

So we haven't talked about it yet, but I'm sure we will. I think my natural tendency would be just to blow it off. I'll get mad and just forget about it. Claudia won't let that happen. She will make me talk about it. That's just how she is. That can be very engaging. And sometimes it can make me very mad—although I've gotten used to it. But sometimes she'll get heavily on my case about not being open enough. And I tend to be a very private person. But Claudia will push you to the limit of what you're willing to talk about. And on some level, over the course of my life, I've come to appreciate that, because I've talked with her about more things than I ever would with anybody else.

Yet for all of Claudia's desire for Nancy to open up and reveal more of herself, sometimes it is she that withdraws:

I know that Claudia will always be my friend. We'll work things out. She'll get mad at me, or I'll get mad at her, but we'll make contact again. Sometimes she pulls away from people for long periods of time. The worst she's ever done is something like six months. And when she does that, it's not out of anger or anything. It's just her style. Some of it is she's really busy, like I am, like most people are, but she also went through a period of depression, and that was probably a piece of it. She just needed to deal with the stuff that was very proximal and close to her—physically close to her. And during those periods, I call her and leave a message, or send her e-mail. I get mad, but I always know she'll reconnect. There are some people that you think just don't want to be your friend. I never think that with Claudia. It would never even cross my mind that she doesn't want to be my friend anymore.

And, finally, as is invariably the case in women's friendships, it all comes down to the magnificence and luxury of talking with your friend—talking and talking and talking:

We meet about once a month and do dinner. We drink, we talk. We sit some place for a long time. When we talk, and when I have dinner with her, it's different than having dinner with other people. It's a conversation that touches me much more, though I can have wonderful conversations with other people. It's just that deeper connectedness. I could sit there for hours. I'm not bored, ever. There's not a lull. It's just different.

Lisa

Nancy sets the stage for the story of her friendship with Lisa far differently than she did for Claudia's story. First, whereas she began the earlier stories by relating difficulties in her friendship with Claudia, here she initially paints a very positive picture of both Lisa and their relationship. Also, she introduces a key theme played out repeatedly in their friendship: until the recent years of their friendship, Nancy was Lisa's boss:

> I've known Lisa thirteen years. Is it that long now? I actually hired her. I guess I was twenty-six. I was just promoted to be supervisor on my unit, so there had to be someone who would replace me, and that was Lisa. She was hired when she was twenty-two. Our original relationship was that I was her supervisor. But there's something similar about us, and what began to happen quite soon was that there was a certain complement. I would always take the lead and she would follow whatever I did and wanted to do. There was a certain synchrony in our work. When we did stuff together, it clicked. Our relationship was different than others involving people that I supervised. Someone else was hired at the same time as Lisa, when I was first promoted. So I was supervising the two of them. And other people would comment that, though this other woman was lovely, there was just a difference in how I worked with Lisa.
>
> She in no way tried to take advantage because she was my friend. She loves what she does, and she enhanced my ability to do my job, because she actually did more. We accomplished much, much more as a team than I ever could have accomplished supervising some other people. And people started to confuse us for one another, even though we really don't look alike.
>
> When I first hired Lisa, she was doing a daytime program and ran a movie on certain nights for emotionally disturbed children. I would show up sometimes at night and help her. She was twenty-two, and that seemed overwhelming to me. I was only a few years older, but nonetheless. . . . So the experiences we'd have together were kind of intense. You'd have these great common experiences and these funny stories. We could laugh for hours about them. So I would make her leave there, and we'd go out and have a drink, and we'd laugh and talk.

Once Nancy has set the stage for me to have a first impression of Lisa as a good friend and co-worker, she goes on to tell me of the problems they have had:

> But we've also had some difficulties. There was this woman Doreen, who I also hired. What Doreen basically did is she wedged herself between Lisa and myself. And Lisa got sucked into it. From my perspective, she aligned herself with Doreen, and actually I think from her perspective she would say the same thing. She pulled very much away from me and towards Doreen. There was some incident where Doreen did something really horrible. And it was very clear that this was not some kind of interpersonal relationship problem between Doreen and me that everybody else could wipe their hands clean of. It was very clear that Doreen had done something awful—and that I had done nothing. And it was very clear to Lisa that her pulling away from me and toward Doreen was wrong. Our friendship was hurt by that.
>
> But a piece of that is just Lisa. Lisa gets torn. Doreen is a very wealthy woman, who basically in many ways bought Lisa. She invited her places that Lisa didn't want to turn down. So our friendship shifted a lot as a result. We went from being very good friends who worked very tightly, to having a more tense type of friendship. We were still friends, but there were very clear boundaries. And I just

started to think, "Well, this is clearly Lisa. She's not going to give up going to these places with Doreen, because Doreen will pay for it. She's just not. So our friendship is going to be different." We would have a work friendship, but that was it. But then after a while we started talking. I guess it took about a year and half. We talked a whole lot. I guess her way of dealing with it was she talked down Doreen a lot. I wouldn't say a word. Doreen has a lot of problems and Lisa would talk about them. That appeared to be her way of making amends. And over time we became very friendly again. And then Doreen quit, so that helped at work. We still weren't as close as we were before, but over time that also shifted.

My guess is that for Lisa, there's still stuff there. But I don't talk about it. She'll bring it up. She in many ways wants me to like Doreen. And I never will. She'll bring Doreen up at times to see what my perception is, to see what I'm thinking. And to see if that's all over with and she can forget about it. It would just make her life easier if that were the case. I don't think it makes all that much difference anymore, because I can't think of any good reasons for our paths to cross. If she had a party, Doreen and I both might go, but it honestly wouldn't be an issue for me. Although it still might be an issue for Lisa.

So Nancy believes that the incident is behind them. She says that she no longer harbors resentment. She goes on to tell me about the positive changes that occurred in their work relationship, resulting from her desire to make sure that Lisa did not feel that their status was unequal:

As we both got older, there had to be a shift in our work relationship, especially when she was promoted. I can remember we had a long talk about how I was her supervisor and she looked up to how I did things that worked. But now she was my equal. So the relationship had to be restructured. And when she got her master's, there was a strain on our personal relationship. I could feel that she had begun to think differently, so I brought that up to her. I felt that we really couldn't be friends and grow, or even grow as colleagues, if she had to do what she thought I wanted as opposed to taking a side road if that's what she felt like she needed to do. Because I could follow her a little ways, or we could complement each other in a new way. So I guess my role with Lisa is I have read her more like Claudia has read me. But then at other times, Lisa has read me very well. There have been times when I haven't said things, and she's just kind of known. And at difficult times for me she has reached out.

Nancy then relates another incident involving Lisa and a mutual co-worker:

The woman who was my supervisor at the time—Valerie—was pretty crazy. She said I was her best friend, which was a scary thing, because we never did dinner, we never did anything. But one day she decided I was getting too powerful and I wasn't supporting her. So she went for the Lisa split. She made Lisa go to lunch with her right before Lisa and I were supposed to do this major presentation. Lisa knew she was supposed to be with me setting up, but she didn't know how to tell Valerie that. She showed up five minutes before the presentation was supposed to start, and I was ready to just strangle her. But that was just the beginning of Valerie getting more and more paranoid about me. So I ended up quitting.

That was a very tough time for me. Another friend stood up for me during that period, but Lisa just couldn't. On some level, I didn't tell Lisa outright what I needed from her. I didn't quite know how to do it. I could see her getting caught up in her own stuff. She was caught in what was good for her career versus our friendship. And I didn't give her the benefit of the doubt and let her work it out. I felt like this is her problem, and she's got to decide what she's going to do here. I just said, "Fine, you deal with your career," and didn't tell her how I was feeling. And Lisa kept on coming over trying to say things like, "You know, I want help here." She was trying to make clear the depth of her friendship to me. And in some place I didn't give her the opportunity.

But she still remained loyal, just like with the Doreen incident. She's loyal in her own way. She's not turning her back. You can see her stuck there. Like with Doreen, I knew the whole time this was going on that it was very difficult for Lisa. But I wasn't going to save her from it, because this was her stuff, not mine. But some people could just drop you and not think. And not be connected. She never was like that. So Lisa does stand by you no matter what, but within her limitations. And I think over time those limitations have lessened. Hopefully, they'll continue to lessen with more life. And I think they have. How she is now, is very different than how she was seven or eight years ago. And the incident with Doreen was ten years ago, eleven years ago.

Claudia and Lisa

The story of Nancy's best friendships ends somewhat as it began—with an explanation of why these two women are her *best* friends:

Lisa and Claudia are very different. Not in how I feel about them. I love them both. But Lisa has a little Doris Day look. Claudia couldn't be more opposite to that. I mean Claudia dresses very nicely and she's lovely. She's very attractive. But Claudia is very flip. And Lisa's very sweet. Sweet would not be a word anybody would ever use to describe Claudia. Lots of people describe Lisa as very sweet and fragile. Claudia is neither. Claudia's extraordinarily robust and has a powerful presence. Lisa can have power, but it's always in a vulnerable, sweet sort of way. And I think I have elements of both of them. I think Lisa and I look very different and can act very different, but there's something about us that's similar that would make people call me Lisa and her Nancy. But I don't have the same level of sweetness that Lisa has or the same level of fragility. In college, Claudia was the outgoing outrageous person. Everybody liked her or was intimidated by her. People thought she was really cool. And when I lived with her, people always wondered how I got to live in that house, because I was the nice girl. People didn't understand. But someone like Lisa would never be in a place like that. There's just something middle-of-the-road adaptable about me that would make me feel close to these two very different types of people.

But they're both warm, engaging, fun friends. And they're very loyal. For instance, Lisa put herself out to make sure that people remembered what I'd set up at work and that I want to do my research there. Even though she's leaving, she's going to come back and be the supervisor of the group I want to observe. She made all kinds of connections for me with new people so that it was easy for me to walk in and do it. So it's nice, because a piece of it is that she's doing it because she knows it will close a chapter for me.

Lisa and Claudia both really know me. They have a good sense of me when I'm with them. They're very attuned to my feelings. I probably have to say less than I have to say to other people. They wouldn't miss my being hurt or being tense about something. They would pick it up. And I think that they're pretty on target about what interests me, and both of them could probably engage me very quickly. I have another good friend, Laura, who I know I can always count on. She would always be there for me. But even though I see her all the time, the friendship is not as deep as it is with Claudia or Lisa. We have less in common. We're less attuned to each other. For instance, if I'm in a bad mood, there could be this huge distance between us that is going to be very hard for either one of us to figure out how to cross, where that's not true with a friend who you're closer with.

FURTHER REFLECTIONS:
A QUESTION OF LOYALTY

When I was interviewing Nancy, I was surprised to hear her say that loyalty was a defining aspect of best friendship for her. On several occasions, she said that Claudia and Lisa are both very loyal. Although all of the women I talked to very likely consider loyalty to be an important aspect of their friendships, Nancy was the only one to use that particular term. I find this so striking because Lisa's actions in the stories involving Doreen and Valerie seem at first glance to be blatantly *dis*loyal.

I struggled with this paradox for some time. I had difficulty understanding how Nancy could place such emphasis on loyalty and still consider Lisa a best friend. Perhaps even more puzzling was that Nancy *described* Lisa as loyal. When I interviewed Nancy the second time, I asked her more about what loyalty meant to her, but I continued to have trouble understanding this whole issue. I began to realize that my difficulty was stemming from my own particular definitions of loyalty and friendship, rather than some inconsistency within Nancy. I needed to let go of my feeling that Lisa was not a loyal, trustworthy friend and explore why Nancy felt she was.

One of the things I did at times to help me better understand portions of an interview was to write it in verse—like a poem. I would listen to the tape of that section as I read along on the transcript, making slashes on the page at each audible pause. I would then rewrite the passage in poem-form, with each slash signifying the end of a line. This technique enabled me to hear the words in new ways by giving me a fresh perspective. I found it to be enormously helpful in understanding Nancy's friendship with Lisa. I used it on a section in which Nancy tells me about the relationships she and Lisa had with Doreen, as well as on one in which I ask Nancy to describe what she means about loyalty.

The following are excerpts from the first of those poems, followed by a discussion. The full texts of the poems can be found in Appendixes B and C:

1 I guess like in a nut
2 shell
3 what happened was
4 I was
5 a supervisor.
6 Um
7 and Lisa—
8 this woman Doreen also
9 you know
10 I hired her and she also worked with us.
11 Um
12 what had happened is Doreen
13 had a lot of problems at work.
14 What Doreen basically did
15 is she wedged herself
16 between Lisa and myself.
17 And Lisa got sucked into it
18 and
19 she
20 uh
21 she
22 she a—
23 from my perspective
24 she aligned herself with Doreen
25 and actually I think from her perspective
26 she'd say the same thing she pulled very much away from me
27 and towards Doreen.

The poem begins with Nancy presenting Doreen as the villain: Doreen actively worked to break up the friendship between Nancy and Lisa, and later she did something "awful" at work to Nancy (ll. 28–60). Nancy and, to a large extent, Lisa appear to be the victims of Doreen. In Nancy's view, Lisa is a victim both of Doreen and of her own weaknesses. For instance, when Doreen "wedges" herself between the two of them, "Lisa got sucked into it" (l. 17). Later when she describes why Lisa pulled away from her and toward Doreen, she says:

83   Doreen is a
84   you know
85   she is a very wealthy woman
86   who basically
87   in many ways
88   bought Lisa.
89   She
90   invited her places
91   that Lisa
92   didn't want to turn down.
93   So [Lisa] was
94   "what should I do here?
95   You know
96   [Doreen] has all these
97   you know she's very wealthy and I can go here
98   or I can
99   do this."

Although Nancy's words could sound judgmental, her tone is rather matter of fact. She seems to be explaining why Lisa felt torn, so that I might understand it as she does. As she explains: "but you know a piece of that is just Lisa/Lisa gets torn" (ll. 78–79). Thus, Lisa behaved the way she did because it is a part of her character not to be sure about the right course of action. Nancy must accept this trait if she is to have Lisa in her life.

That is not to say, however, that Nancy places no blame with Lisa. Nor is it to say that she views Lisa as entirely passive. She sees that Lisa actively "aligned herself with Doreen" and "she pulled very much away from me/and towards Doreen" (ll. 24 and 26-27). Nancy also describes herself as becoming quite angry as a result of Lisa's actions. Over time, however, Nancy and Lisa found a way to mend the wounds in their friendship. Nancy forgave Lisa and came to understand that Lisa regretted her actions.

I do not think this episode alone would have caused me to question Nancy's definition of loyalty. Certainly, a loyal friend can make an error in judgment. However, there is that second episode, this time involving Valerie. Further, it turns out that Doreen is not entirely out of the picture. She and Lisa are still friends, despite the fact that, together, they hurt Nancy. It is this aspect of the story that I found difficult to understand. How can Lisa maintain ties with Doreen? And how can Nancy accept that state of affairs? Although it is apparent that Nancy recognizes that there are difficulties in Lisa and Doreen's relationship—and perhaps she finds consolation in this—it still seemed to me that Lisa's disloyalty to Nancy is ongoing by the very fact that she and Doreen are still friends.

The second poem resulted from my attempt to understand what loyalty means to Nancy. The following is an excerpt:

61 "So how would you define loyalty—"
62 —how would I define loyalty?
63 "—in a friendship?"
64 Um
65 I don't know
66 I guess like, well—
67 loyalty is
68 I don't know
69 like in a friend
70 it's someone who is always your friend no matter what.
71 Um
72 and it's someone
73 who
74 will
75 stand by you no matter what.
76 Um
77 I guess what I'm saying about Lisa
78 is she'll s—
79 she does
80 stand by you no matter what
81 but within her limitations.

————————————————

150 "OK. So it's a trait that you feel that you have, as well."
151 Yeah. Towards them?
152 "Yeah."
153 Yes, you know yes.
154 Well I think
155 in general
156 I think I'm a very loyal person.
157 But I think
158 when you talk about loyalty in friendship
159 um
160 there's a depth to that
161 that you have
162 with different people.
163 You know, like
164 um
165 there are many people
166 you know
167 I would say
168 I very much care about and am being loyal to
169 but under certain circumstances
170 if I hadda choose
171 I'd be conflicted
172 about how much I have to give
173 But then there's a group of people
174 who
175 it doesn't matter
176 how much I have to give
177 'cause that's what I need to do
178 because they're my
179 very good friends.

In this passage, Nancy tries to explain to me how she can consider Lisa loyal in light of the stories she has told me. Although she could have felt defensive when I essentially challenged her concept of a friend, that is not the tone she takes. Instead, she seems to understand my confusion and seeks to clear it up. It feels to me throughout this piece that she knows what she means when she says that Lisa is loyal. She is attempting only to make *me* understand.

Throughout the section, Nancy describes ways in which Lisa is loyal by giving me examples of things Lisa would *not* do:

> while all this is going on
> like she's not
> turning her back (ll. 10-12).

> you know she's not someone who would ever lie
> or
> she's not underhanded
> she doesn't gossip (ll. 26-29).

> but like she just didn't
> like some people could just like
> drop you and not think.
> And like not be connected.
> She never I—I—
> she never was like that (ll. 55-60).

Thus, Nancy sees Lisa as loyal because Lisa does not turn her back, gossip, do underhanded things, or drop Nancy altogether. But in her first definition of loyalty in a friendship, Nancy says that a friend is loyal when she "stands by you no matter what" (ll. 68-75). Yet, that is exactly what Lisa does not seem to do—she does not stand by Nancy no matter what. But Nancy goes on to say, presumably sensing the inherent contradiction in her words:

> Um
> I guess what I'm saying about Lisa
> is she'll s—
> she does
> stand by you no matter what
> but within her limitations (ll. 76-81).

Earlier, Nancy says: "like she's a very good friend/but she gets tied up" (ll. 30-31). Thus, as indicated above, Lisa is a victim, to some extent, of her own character flaws. Nancy describes her in these poems as confused, torn, stuck, and searching for a way to deal with her conflict. She wants to be a good friend. She wants to do the right thing but sometimes she just *cannot* do it.

Nancy's way of reconciling her feelings about loyalty with Lisa's actions is based on an overall approach Nancy has to friendship. Once she accepts people into her life, she does not spend a lot of time questioning why they are the way they are or wishing they could be different. For example, at one point in the second interview I ask her how she feels about the fact that Claudia tends to probe a great deal and pushes Nancy to be more open. She replies:

> What do you mean what do I feel about it? I don't know, Claudia's a very good friend of mine. So . . . it certainly makes me feel uncomfortable and I'll laugh about it. I don't know it's . . . I don't know what to say.

Later I ask, "Do you like that she does that?"

> I don't know, I guess. You know, it's just . . . our relationship. And Claudia's been my friend since I was seventeen . . . and it's just who she is. I wouldn't say I like it or it's not like I dislike it, it's—it would be somebody different.

When I, in an attempt to clarify her meaning, start to ask, "So you just sort of accept what—," Nancy interrupts me: "Well, its not that I accept it, it's just who she is. . . . " Nancy was somewhat annoyed and baffled by my inability to understand what she was saying. My questions made little sense to her because of the way she constructs her friendships. It is not a question of whether Nancy likes or accepts a particular characteristic of her friend: Claudia is who she is. Likewise, with Lisa, she accepts that Lisa has limitations and therefore cannot always be as loyal as other friends. Furthermore, it is more important to Nancy that Lisa *wants* to be loyal—that she *wants* to do the right thing—than that she always succeeds:

> Like you can see it in her face
> that she's connected
> and that she doesn't know what to do.
> Like she's trying to find a way (ll. 14-17).

Lisa is simply doing her best—and that is enough for Nancy.

Chapter 4

Liz

Liz is a twenty-eight-year-old white woman, living alone in a studio apartment and studying for her doctorate. She is engaged to be married, although she and her fiancé have not yet set a date for the wedding. Both interviews took place in her apartment. I sat on a couch, with my recording equipment on a coffee table in front of me, and she sat on her bed facing me.

Liz immediately put me at ease with her relaxed and friendly style. Although she talked quite freely, there were times during the first interview when it felt as if she was not being completely open about certain topics. She would refer to events somewhat obliquely and not elaborate on details. I was not sure at the time if she was being guarded or if she thought the information she had left out would not be of interest to me.

At the end of that interview, after I had turned off my tape recorder, Liz mentioned to me that she had a theory about women's friendships. I told her that I would definitely want to explore her ideas further in the next interview. She said that she had not mentioned them earlier because she did not know if her ruminations would be of interest to me. I explained that they were and told her that I would greatly appreciate it if she would write down any further thoughts she might have before the next interview. Toward the end of the second interview, I asked Liz about her theory. She talked for several minutes about her beliefs regarding the impact competition has on women's friendships. I do not include Liz's theories in her narrative, because they are not an integral part of the story of her friendships. However, Liz's thoughts on this topic served as something of a starting point for my analysis of competitive feelings among best friends (see Chapter 5).

THE STORY

Susan

Of the five women interviewed who have two best friends, Liz is the only one who chooses to begin our interviews talking about the friendship that she formed more recently. Liz's divergence in this respect alerted me to another characteristic that was, in fact, universal among all the friendships the women presented first: they were the friendships the participants described as closer, or more intimate.

I particularly like the way Liz begins her story of her friendship with Susan, because she talks about her first impression upon seeing Susan. In one study looking at how women make friends, the researchers found that as women make their way through the world, they continually filter out potential "friend candidates" using first impressions, because they have a "friendship budget" that allows one to have only so many friends at one time.[1] Although most of us have heard throughout our lives that we must never judge a book by its cover—and we may even subscribe to that adage—we also do just that in subtle or not so subtle ways all the time. Fortunately for Liz, she had ample opportunity within her dormitory setting to overcome her initial reaction to Susan:

> I met Susan on my first day of college. She lived across the hall from me. When I first saw her, I was a little bit surprised by her. She was from the city. And I'm from a very small town. So she looked kind of different than people that I was used to seeing, in her dress and the way she carried herself. And I remember being very intrigued, but kind of intimidated by her at the same time. I remember thinking, "Oh, she's so streetwise. She must be really knowledgeable about things." I think, too, I was feeling a little bit insecure about being from this small town and going to college and fitting in. And she just seemed so worldly at the time.
>
> A few days later we just happened to be out in the hall talking, and I remember being surprised at how nice she was. She was a lot nicer than I thought she would be. I guess I thought she was going to be this really hard person, and she wasn't. And we just started hanging out and became very good friends. As I got to know her, I realized that she was a lot like me, even though we had different backgrounds. And yet we both have always really recognized how different we are from one another. People used to say to us all the time, "I can't believe you two are friends." Or, "I can't believe you guys hang out." And actually one year we dressed up like each other for Halloween, because we're just so different in our appearance. We're like two extremes.

Liz clearly revels in some of the differences between Susan and her. She goes on to talk briefly about some of the ways the relationship has evolved since college:

> The friendship has definitely changed over time, through the different stages of our lives. I would say that from college to after college, when we were living in the same city, the friendship was pretty much the same, in that it was a major social outlet and a major support system. And now we live apart. But I think the major difference is that we both have serious relationships—we're both engaged to get married. And so in some ways our roles for each other have changed. There's another person in the picture who is providing support. So I wouldn't say the roles have been replaced, but they're kind of shared now. I still feel like she and I have an intimacy that's separate and special from the one she has with her fiancé, but now my role as a support system is shared with him.

Liz goes on to talk about what Susan is like, beginning with what she admires and gradually revealing aspects of her friend she has more trouble with:

> Susan's very together and very independent. She's artistic and creative. I think the thing I admire most about her is that she carries herself with this incredible confidence that makes her very noticeable. I think she's very comfortable with who she is and how she looks and the way she presents herself. I think that works really well for her. And she has a very good head on her shoulders. She's very insightful. She's a really good person to talk to when you have a problem. She really seems to be able to look at a problem objectively. Kind of stand back from it and give a point of view that's very real, that's not slanted. She's not afraid to just tell you how she feels and how she sees it. And I'm always amazed at how often she'll say something and I'll just ignore it, and then she'll turn out to be absolutely right. And then I'll have to say, "Oh, well you were right about that. You called it." So she's very perceptive.
>
> Susan is also very sensitive and considerate. She's very sensitive to her own feelings and to the feelings of others. And because of that I think she always tries to be very accommodating, sometimes to a fault in terms of sacrificing herself for the needs of others. And, in fact, sometimes I find that side of her really frustrating. Sometimes she just can't say no, and she just lets people walk all over her. For instance, there's this girl we were both friends with in college. And she just totally took advantage of Susan. And even though she did all these things to Susan, this girl will still call her and say, "Oh I need this. Do you mind doing this? Can I come visit?" and Susan will say, "Sure." If it were me, I would say, "Absolutely not and don't ever speak to me again." But in some ways she just can't say no. We've actually discussed this. She says it's because her standards are not as high as mine. But I think that's bullshit. I think it's ridiculous. I think that's her way of justifying. And I feel very much like, "Look, when are you going to draw the line with this girl?"
>
> It's the same thing with Andy, her cousin. They grew up together and are very close. He's a drug addict, and she just lets him run all over her. He's abusive toward her—emotionally and physically. Sometimes I can't understand why she

just can't say, "Enough." But she won't. I understand that it's different for her—he's her cousin. But my feeling is that he's done some things that, as far as I'm concerned, are not forgivable. I will not ever have any type of relationship with him, ever. And Susan and I have had arguments about how she lets him treat her. I mean it's terrible for her, and when it's terrible for her, I feel it too. I can feel her pain. But yet I'm kind of powerless to make her do something about it.

My first real run-in with her cousin was in college, when he came to visit us. Susan and I were rooming together in a dorm room, and he was supposed to stay for two days. He stayed for a week and in the meantime managed to be incredibly rude to me. But also managed to have Susan running around like a chicken with her head cut off. He was out of control. He was drunk nonstop in our room. And there were a couple of nights that he didn't even come home. And Susan didn't know where he was, and he didn't know where he was, and so she was worried sick.

I think she feels like she has no control with him. Like with that incident, it was totally out of her hands. So when it's 1:00 in the morning and I have an exam and I'm trying to study, and he's in our room drinking and has been since noon, and she's sitting there too, she really feels like she can't do anything. I ended up taking all his stuff and throwing it outside and telling him he had to leave and that he was not to come back. She had never seen me so enraged before, and I think she was scared, but I think she also knew that she had totally lost control of the situation, and she needed me to take control. So she was also relieved, but didn't really recognize it at first.

But of course it's her cousin, so she's a lot more forgiving than I am. Like now, he just moved in with her. She's getting married, and he and his alcoholic wife just moved into her new house. I think it's terrible, a disaster. But Susan's really protective of him, because he has a serious problem. And she'll take a lot of abuse from him. But I won't ever forgive him—or have a relationship with him.

Liz is open about times when things have not been good between Susan and her. In particular, she relates a story from their college days that sheds light on aspects of their relationship:

Susan and I have had some difficulties, but we've always confronted them. Well, I guess I've confronted them more than she has. She has a lot more difficulty dealing with her feelings than I do. She tends to keep her problems bottled up inside, while I tend to express my feelings more openly. Sometimes some hurt feelings have resulted from us sort of taking each other for granted. This was particularly true when we first lived far apart. We had really depended on each other so much until that point in time. And somehow when we started living further apart there were ways in which we were being insensitive, in that we recognized that there was a really strong bond, but we were taking it for granted. So we talked about how close we feel to one another and perhaps how that leads to some arguments or hurt feelings.

And there was a time in college when I was really unhappy and I was taking that out on her. Her reaction was basically to ignore it and not confront it. I actually was the one that kind of confronted the fact that, "Gee, I've been treating you really badly." Later, she told me that she felt like she didn't know what was going on with me and didn't know how to confront it. So she just decided to let it go and figured that when I was ready to talk about it I would. But in some ways I think I would have liked her to confront me so I would have been able to confide in her a little bit more than I was able to at the time.

But I don't know, I was just really unhappy, so it was hard for me to even tell her what was going on with me. I was just unhappy at school and I didn't want to be there. I was having a really hard time with my boyfriend from home. All during college we had agreed to have an open relationship and date other people, because we wanted to have fun. And then when I found out he was seeing someone else, I felt very threatened. I actually had been dating a guy at school who Susan and I are both very, very good friends with, but he and I had ended our relationship. And, at that time, I wanted to go into an honors program and it wasn't working out, in terms of where I needed to be with credits. I had thought of studying abroad and I couldn't do the honors program if I wanted to do that.

Another thing was that Susan was dating this guy named Earl, who was just a sweetheart. It was very difficult in a lot of ways, to see that relationship blossom when my relationship with Jeff was in the toilet and my relationship with Paul was pretty much over. And actually Paul had started dating another friend of mine. So I felt just bad about everything. I was really depressed. I guess it was the loneliest I've ever felt. I think in a lot of ways I just couldn't talk about it. Susan wanted to be there for me, but I didn't want to talk about it.

She was leaving that next semester to go elsewhere to study. She and Earl were going together, and they were making plans. It was really nice, and I'm actually sorry I couldn't have shared that excitement with her at the time. Part of the problem, too, was that she was actually very happy at that time. When someone's so happy, and you're so miserable, it's like you can't be happy for them. You don't want them to be miserable too, but you kind of wish they weren't so happy. So in a lot of ways I really closed Susan out. And as I mentioned, she just kind of backed away from it. As I said, she's not a big confronter. So I'm not surprised that she didn't confront me. Maybe in some ways I did want her to. But I can't say that she wasn't supportive of me during that time. She was supportive, but in a very superficial way.

So at the end of the semester, I finished my last final, packed up my stuff—I decided to go abroad—and left. And I didn't say goodbye to anyone. I didn't even say goodbye to Susan. But then, after I was away for about a month, I wrote her a letter. And then she wrote me back, saying, "I didn't know what was going on with you. I was really worried." She actually thought maybe it was something she had done, but I think I just really lost sight myself. But going away was very, very good for me, because it really made me see that I could stand on my own and be independent.

And all of a sudden I realized, I really don't need those things that I thought I did—like Jeff and the honors program. But I still really felt like I needed Susan. I wrote to her, and to Sandy. I wrote them constantly while I was there, and they wrote back. I needed that type of emotional support. And the things that I thought were so important all of a sudden didn't seem that important after all.

Liz has had a unique opportunity to see her friendship with Susan through the eyes of others, which has led to further reflection:

Susan and I have a really intimate and a really intense relationship. We can be very emotional with each other. And I feel like we can talk about anything. I guess in some ways it's a very natural friendship. It kind of developed very naturally. We weren't roommates, forced to live together. We lived across the hall from each other and we just started hanging out together, and the friendship just evolved. We're very compatible. It's funny, I never really thought about our friendship much until one time, a year after we graduated college, we went back to get some recommendations from the school. We happened to run into someone we had graduated with. This person came up to us and said something to the effect of, "I'm so glad to see you two together." And then he said something like, "You two are just meant to be together. And I'm so happy that you're living so close and spending so much time together, because it's meant to be that way." And this is someone that I really wasn't very close to, that Susan had more of a relationship with than I did. It kind of took me aback that an outsider who didn't really know me that well, and certainly didn't know our friendship all that well, observed that quality to it. So I guess that was the first time I really thought about it. And in reflecting back on it, I was thinking, "Well, he's right. This is kind of meant to be. This just feels right as a friendship."

It's funny, another reaction we once had to our friendship was that a friend of ours from college had a roommate who thought that Susan and I were lovers. She didn't realize that we were just friends. And this woman who thought this actually also happened to be a lesbian. I was very surprised, because I've never really even considered that . . . it just doesn't exist in our relationship, in my opinion. I just don't have those feelings. And we both felt like, "Oh my God. What are you talking about?" I know that Susan's never felt that way . . . at least she hasn't ever voiced it to me. It's just not there. And when the woman said it, at first I actually thought that my friend she was living with had, as a joke, told her that Susan and I were lovers or something. But I wasn't upset about it. I guess my thought was, "Why would you think that?" And I think that was Susan's too. Like, "What would make you think that?" Not in a defensive way. At least I don't feel like I was defensive about it. But it was more like, "Why do you think that? What would make someone pick up on that?"

So I feel like we have this very tight bond with one another. And that it's a bond that's very solid and it doesn't matter if we're not going to school together—if we live on opposite sides of the country, it's still going to be there. And it's been through some very difficult times too. But I think the difficult times we've had have allowed the friendship to mature. It's been able to become something that I guess in some ways I feel will always just be there. And it's not something that I can honestly say I've ever really doubted. I think Susan has had times where she's doubted it. Like when I threw her cousin out of the room. And then junior year when I was really depressed, she was really worried that I wouldn't want to be friends anymore. But I guess I just always felt like it was going to be there.

Sandy

As Liz switches gears and shares the story of her friendship with Sandy, the differences between a friendship formed in high school and one formed in college emerge. And yet, while there are clear distinctions between her friends and friendships, the words and phrases Liz uses to describe Susan and Sandy and to evoke the closeness she feels to each of them are strikingly similar:

I've known Sandy since the fourth grade. But we didn't really become friends until high school, until ninth grade, when she sat diagonally across from me in a class. It was a class where it was all males, besides Sandy and me. And we really weren't friends, but because we were the only two girls in the class, we sat next to each other and would talk to each other. We developed a very, very close friendship. And in some ways I would say that that friendship changed my whole high school experience. She's very outgoing and was always saying, "Oh, let's go here, let's go there." And it made high school a lot more fun. And then we kept in touch all through college. We saw each other on the holidays, wrote letters back and forth, and really have done that ever since.

Sandy and I have a real sense of connection because we grew up together. We come from the same place, our parents know each other, and my cousin went to high school with her sister. Our families and our backgrounds are very meshed with one another. So I think that gives us a special bond. I feel as if we always have something to talk about. We always have a common ground because of that experience.

Sandy is a really together person. She's very, very confident. And she's incredibly independent. She's probably the most independent person I know. In some ways, she really kind of functions outside of her family. Like for holidays, she'll call up every member of her family, find out what they're doing, decide where she wants to go, and book her ticket based upon that. While if I don't see my parents on a holiday, they'd probably keel over and die or something. But she's very independent in that way. I don't really see her as being emotionally dependent upon anyone. I guess she's very guarded in that respect. But I almost think that she doesn't feel that need in some way. And she really is the type of person that basically does what she wants to pretty much all the time.

In high school, she was actually very emotional. And since college, she doesn't really display emotions anymore. And she always says, "Can you believe I was voted most emotional in high school?" Now she's like a rock. But I don't know if she's really being guarded or if that's just how she's evolved her personality—if it happened because she was really kind of put in a situation of independence. Her parents separated when she was in high school, and her father moved away. And her mother, who's very odd, would just go off and do her own thing. We would come home from school and there would be a note on the table, "Sandy, gone away with a friend. Be back in a week." So she was thrust into a very independent role. She really had no choice. I think that kind of shaped who she's become. I think in some ways that's taught her to be very strong emotionally.

Our understanding of the friendship grows as Liz begins to compare it in her own mind to her other best friendship:

I would say that our relationship is a lot more fun-based than the intimacy I have with Susan. I still feel like we tell each other a lot, and we don't hold things back, but I guess it doesn't have that intense quality that my relationship with Susan has. It's a little bit lighter. I think I tell her the same things I tell Susan, but I don't talk about my feelings quite as in-depth or how things make me feel. It's more, "Oh, this happened and this happened, and can you believe this, and I can't believe it," and like that. But it's not that there isn't an intimacy. There is. It's just different than it is with Susan.

For example, I recently saw Sandy. We had been out drinking, and then we went back to her place. We were getting ready for bed while we were talking. And we were having a very serious conversation, but we were having it in a casual way. We were just going about doing what we were doing while we talked. So I think our relationship is just as intimate as Susan's and mine, but it has this incredibly casual feel. Like we can have this deeply serious and intimate conversation while I'm brushing my teeth, and somehow that seems to work very comfortably. But I can't ever imagine having a conversation with Susan in that manner. With Susan, I think we'd have to sit down and really talk about it, and really focus on it and hash it out.

I think a big part of it is that with Sandy there's a lot less emotion shown behind the feelings. Even though she might really be feeling it, she presents it in a very casual, nonchalant manner, where Susan is much more apt to put her feelings right out there. Not only in words, which is what Sandy does, but to really show the emotions. Sandy is much more controlled. I think my relationship with Susan is much more intense because we reach that higher intensity of emotion, in terms of actual display of emotion. Whereas with Sandy, because she's so controlled, in some ways I guess I feel like I need to be a little more controlled. Not that I think she'd be uncomfortable if I was really emotional or that I think she would not be as consoling, but I think the conversation takes on a different tone with Sandy than it does with Susan.

And although I feel really close to Sandy, I guess sometimes I worry about her. I guess because she's so independent, sometimes I have difficulty with that relationship in that it lacks the recognition you get through knowing that someone needs you. Because she is so much on her own in a lot of ways. So sometimes I find that difficult.

Sandy and I also don't really talk about our relationship. We don't have conflicts or arguments either, probably largely because it isn't as intensely intimate. I can't think of a time when I've been truly angry at her. The only thing we might have is something where I'll just say something quick to her like, "What'd you say that for?" And I can think of times when I've thought, "What is she doing? What is she thinking?" But I've never really felt like that was reflected upon me. It doesn't feel as personal as it does with Susan. Like when I think Susan is being hurt by her cousin and that, in turn, hurts me. I guess I don't feel Sandy's feelings as much I do Susan's.

Susan and Sandy

What emerges most of all as Liz talks more about both of her friends is the sense that these are relationships in which she can just be—there is trust, knowledge, and acceptance:

I can't think of anything I wouldn't tell either Sandy or Susan. They know some very, very private things about me and things, in terms of my relationship with Jeff, that Jeff doesn't even know about. I'm never afraid to tell them anything. No matter how I think it might make me look or how it might be perceived, I'm just not afraid to tell them anything. And in telling them, it makes me feel a lot better for having just said it to someone. And I know I can trust them. There's never a question of that. I know they won't judge me. It's like they know me too well to judge me. The judgments have already been made. And I also know anything I say will remain confidential.

I don't know, though, if I would necessarily tell them everything about them. Like if there was a problem. I don't know if I would . . . it depends what the problem is, but I think I might be a little more reserved in terms of my approach. Or maybe I would say the important things—because I think I have told them all of those things—but maybe not the unimportant things. Like if I thought one of them was getting too heavy, I don't think I'd say, "You're looking heavy." I certainly might be thinking it, but I don't think I would ever say something like that. Unless of course it got to the point where I thought they were being dangerous. And I think there are a couple times when they've decided to do something and I was thinking, "Wow, this is a really bad decision," but I haven't necessarily said anything about it because it was done and there's no point in pouring salt in the wound and saying, "Well that was really stupid."

I think Susan and Sandy both really know me. I think first of all that they're able to read me pretty well. They can tell when I'm uncomfortable or when I'm unhappy, when something's bothering me. And they know my vulnerabilities. For example, when I'm talking about things that are happening to me or what's going on with me, they're able to kind of look at the situation and put it in perspective for me so that I can see it and understand it. They're very good at seeing a situation and offering advice, but also in predicting what might happen, through knowing my vulnerabilities. They say things like, "You know, Liz, that sounds great, sounds like a lot of fun, but you should really be careful of this, or you should really make sure that you don't get too caught up in this." So they present it to me in very gentle terms, but in a way that's very helpful and that's very constructive. So when I say, "I'm going to see so-and-so," Susan will say, "Well, you might want to think about this and how that's going to affect your relationship with Jeff." And these are all things I know, but it helps to have someone say it to me, because I'm really justifying it as this or that, because I want to do it.

I think they also know my boundaries. So they do push my buttons and challenge me when I'm doing something questionable, but they also, I think, know when to back off and when to just say, "This is the way it is." Like Susan knows that I really dislike her ex-boyfriend Joe, so she is in no way going to try to get us to hang out together. I mean she knows not to push me on that topic. She'll tell me if something happens between them—and I usually will hold back my comments and I'll try to be very comforting to her—but she knows not to push me in terms of trying to make me think Joe is a great guy, or trying to convince me that Andy is a model cousin. She knows when enough is enough for me. And Sandy does too. Since we went to high school together, Sandy really knows all the nitty-gritty stuff, like way back to my first boyfriend in ninth grade. And she can tease me a lot about that stuff, but she also knows my limits.

FURTHER REFLECTIONS:
KNOWING WHAT TO SAY AND WHEN TO SAY IT

Over the course of the two interviews I had with Liz, Susan's cousin continually emerged as a significant figure. One of the things that strikes me about this aspect of Liz's story is the depth and range of feelings she has about Susan's relationship with her cousin, as well as how raw those feelings sometimes appear to be. At times she expresses anger and frustration at Susan for allowing her cousin to take advantage of her, and at other times she talks about how painful it is for her to see Susan's being hurt.

There is one piece of the transcript in particular that I find to be especially helpful in shedding light on who Liz is as a friend and the distress she feels as a result of Susan's relationship with her cousin. I initially found this section difficult to code. However, after rewriting it as a poem, much of its meaning opened up for me. (For the entire text of the poem, see Appendix D.) This portion of the transcript follows my having asked Liz about the extent to which she shares with Susan and Sandy. In the first interview, she says that she tells her friends *everything*. In the second interview, I try to probe that further to see if there are indeed areas that she keeps to herself. After thinking for a bit, she says that she might not tell them certain things about themselves—for instance, she does not think she would tell them that they were getting too heavy, if that were the case, unless she became concerned about their health. She then goes on to say:

> I think
> I think there are
> there a couple times when they made really bad decisions.
> And I was thinking,
> "Wow this is a really bad decision,"
> but I haven't necessarily
> said anything about it
> because either
> it was done
> and there's no point of, like,
> pouring salt in the wound and saying,
> "Well, that was really
> you know, stupid,"

So it was either done
or it was something that I felt like
they felt strongly about
I don't agree with
but there's nothing I can do (ll. 1-18).

Liz's words here show her as continually thinking within her friendships—thinking about how her thoughts might affect her friends and her friendships were she to verbalize them. It is evident that she has in mind times when she disagrees with a choice one of her friends has made but has not verbalized her thoughts to the friend. There are two reasons she gives for not doing so. The first, that it is sometimes after the fact, has two parts: (1) It would only hurt them ("pouring salt in the wound"); and (2) There is no use telling them now, because the decision has already been made. Thus, she is protecting them. It is not clear what she does in lieu of telling them what she thinks, but based on other parts of the interview, I can presume that she listens to and supports them.

The second reason she chooses not to tell them is that she feels it is of no use because the disagreement is too great ("there's nothing I can do"). She is speculating that the two of them disagree to such a degree that it can serve no purpose to confront her friend. Doing so would lead to a verbal disagreement—as opposed to the nonverbal one that presumably exists—and it would not change her friend's mind. Also embedded in this piece is a juxtaposition between *thinking* and *feeling*. Liz has *thoughts* about her friends' decisions that are presented alongside her *feelings* about her friends' feelings ("or it was something that I felt like they felt strongly about").

Liz then goes on to present a current example of what she has been talking about:

Like actually right now
Susan's cousin
just moved in with her
and I think this is like a *disaster.*
I think it's *terrible*
Um
but I really don't feel like I can say to her
"This is *terrible*" (laughing ironically).

Although I
I absolutely feel that way (ll. 19-27).

She *thinks* that Susan's decision to allow her cousin to live with her
is a terrible one, but this is again played out against her *feeling* that
she cannot tell Susan what she thinks.

I ask Liz if she thinks Susan knows how she feels. She says that Susan does. The question then emerges: If Liz knows that Susan is
aware of Liz's beliefs about Susan's cousin's moving in with her, why
does Liz resist verbalizing those thoughts to Susan? She is not protecting her from anything, according to Liz, that Susan does not already know. Liz's refrain about her feelings about Susan's decision is
repeated several times during the poem. Toward the end, she repeats
that Susan knows that Liz thinks it is a terrible decision, even though
Liz has not verbalized her thoughts (ll. 70-77). And then Liz provides
an answer as to why she has not shared her beliefs with Susan, even
though she is sure Susan knows what they are:

> Because
> I just think that it's (sighing)
> you know it's happening regardless
> and I think
> she's in some ways
> I mean I think she
> has so many issues
> with her cousin
> that
> I think it would just make things worse if I
> you know said to her
> "This is terrible."
> Because I think she probably knows it
> but I don't think wants to believe it (ll. 78-92).

Thus, she does not want to compound the problem. She does not want
to make Susan feel worse. Liz understands that not only does Susan
know how Liz feels, Susan also likely knows the real truth—that her
decision to let her cousin move in *is* a terrible one.

The last part of the poem begins with Liz momentarily suggesting
the possibility that maybe things will work out. But she does not
really believe that: "But/I'm not bettin' on it" (ll. 96-97), which she

accompanies with an ironic laugh. And finally Liz explains that all that she has just told me is "a prime example of something I really feel like I cannot/say/anything to her about" (ll. 99-101). But, ultimately, that may be all right, because Susan "knows it." "It" may be the truth about what Liz thinks or the truth about Susan's decision to allow her cousin to move in (the truth being that it is a bad decision) or both. Throughout the poem, Liz seems to be struggling—struggling to explain her thought processes to me, struggling with her feelings about Susan's decision, and struggling with her own decision not to tell Susan how she feels.

Liz's depth of emotion about Susan's relationship with her cousin provides a window into all that Liz puts into her closest friendships. She works hard within them, worrying, thinking, caring. She searches for the way to be the best friend she can be. We see this in particular in stark relief against her decision not to have a relationship with Andy. To be in a relationship requires an energy for Liz that she refuses to expend on Susan's cousin.

Chapter 5

"Although Sometimes My Friends Are Competitive, I Don't Think I Ever Am": Navigating Choppy Waters

I played competitive tennis for most of my pre-adult life. I was a good player. I quit early in my senior year of college, when I felt I had lost my "competitive edge." I never defined that term for myself, but I always knew I had it up until that point. I think it had to do with an ability to stay focused during a match. It required a great desire to win, a confidence in my ability to do so, even when faced with a match point against me, and—perhaps most of all—a temporary but very real dislike of whomever was across the net. For that reason, I was never happy playing important matches against people I liked off the court. In particular, I hated playing friends.

As fate would have it, my best friend during high school was also my greatest tennis rival. We vied for the number one spot on our team, we played in the finals of the State tournament, and we played year in and year out in our city tournament. Sometimes she won and sometimes I won. We never talked about the competitiveness that permeated our relationship—both on the court and off—and I never thought it affected us. But it doubtless contributed to the disintegration of our friendship during our senior year of high school.

Although it has been close to twenty years since I stepped onto a court with her, a memory of a handful of matches we played has stayed with me. We are in the middle of a match. I am playing well. I am focused on each point and on my own game. I am not thinking about my opponent or on what effect my winning will have on her or on our relationship. I am, in fact, winning. But as is often the case in close female friendships, my friend knows me. So as we are switching sides between games, she talks to me. She makes a joke. She forces me to connect with her. She makes me see her for more than just my opponent. Consciously or unconsciously, she knows that my will—my competitive edge—cannot withstand her efforts. I laugh with her. And I lose the match. I did not know how to navigate the choppy waters resulting from trying simultaneously to take care of the relationship and to remain competitive. I am not sure I would be any more successful today.

Competitiveness is a difficult issue for women, particularly when it emerges in their closest relationships. The women I talked with are no exception. In particular, it is a recurrent theme in the narratives of Nancy, Linda, and Liz. But each woman has a slightly different take on its role in their lives and relationships, and on their feelings about it. Nancy believes that competitive feelings have emerged in both of her best friendships, but that those feelings have emanated from her friends, not from her. She also believes that openly acknowledging those feelings with one of her friends has led to a strengthening of the bond between them. In contrast, Linda states that no competitive feelings exist in her two friendships. She believes this is the case in large part because she, herself, is not competitive. She also emphasizes that competition and close friendship cannot coexist. Liz, like Linda, feels that her friendships are devoid of competitive feelings. However, she believes that competition between women is the norm and that her two friendships were able to develop specifically because there was no reason for such feelings to emerge.

NANCY

> And then there were some competitions. Although I don't know if there were competitions, I never actually perceived it that way.

Nancy brings up competitive feelings in her friendship with Claudia early in our first interview, after describing how she and Claudia first met and became friends. The contradiction inherent in the quotation above points to her apparent discomfort in discussing those competitive feelings. Although competition is one of the first things that comes to mind for Nancy as she begins to tell me the story of her friendship with Claudia, she immediately refutes her statement. She reacts to her own words as if she has touched a hot stove.

In the anecdote that follows that statement, Nancy tells me about the incident during their freshman year of college in which Claudia had expected and told her friends that she would be asked to the spring dance by a classmate named David. Instead, David asked Nancy, and Claudia was quite disappointed. Nancy does not describe feeling badly that she was asked instead of Claudia. Although she says she was concerned about Claudia's feelings should she decide to go with David, she emphasizes that Claudia had told everybody that David was going to ask her, thereby indicating, I thought, that Claudia was somewhat responsible for her own hurt feelings.

Later, Nancy relates the incident in which she and Claudia were the only students in a class to pass a test. Nancy describes Claudia as usually not caring about grades because "she was the most popular person in the class." But in this case, when she turned out to have the 92 she was quite pleased. As Nancy relates it, Claudia walked over to where Nancy was sitting, apparently confident that Nancy had failed: "And I could tell that—I knew she was thinking that I failed." Although Nancy does not say so explicitly, she seems to be saying that Claudia came over to gloat. When Nancy then continues, "And I had the 96," it feels as if *she* is doing the same. The picture Nancy paints of this incident is vivid. The pleasure that she apparently derived from how it played out is palpable. Even if Nancy did not set out to compete with Claudia in this instance, as in the last, in the face of what she interpreted as Claudia's competitiveness, she clearly became competitive.

Nancy offers these stories as examples of how her friendship with Claudia was strengthened by their ability to confront and work through their difficulties. But it seems important to note that both stories end with Nancy as the winner. Her very renderings have a competitive tenor. She presents herself as a passive party, reluctantly drawn into competition with Claudia and always winning despite herself. Yet, there is a satisfaction in her words, "But he asked me" and "And I had the 96." Both, although only the second explicitly so, are set against a background in which Nancy perceives Claudia to be an extraordinarily popular and charismatic figure at the college. Thus, she comes out ahead in these two instances, even if, overall, Claudia is the more popular of the two.

Although Nancy does acknowledge that these anecdotes are, in part, about competitive feelings, she finds it difficult to admit in the

context of the interviews that *she* has any of those feelings. Before relating the second anecdote, she says, "I guess there was a lot of competition and conflict going on with grades and stuff. . . . And we ended
up talking a whole lot about competition, primarily on her side. At
least I wasn't so aware of it." Nancy implies that the competitive feelings in the relationship have been almost entirely Claudia's. However, she acknowledges that she may have feelings of which she is not
altogether aware.

The next time competition comes up is toward the end of the second interview. Nancy has been talking about her working relationship
with Lisa. She tells me that Lisa always enhanced her ability to do her
job. I then bring up the subject of competition by asking her: "Has
there ever been any feeling of competition?" She replies:

> When she went for her master's, I guess there was a brief period
> where she needed to grow a lot. There was a supervisory posi-
> tion that opened in another department, and she decided to go
> for that. And I helped her speak to the person in charge so that
> she could maintain part of her practice . . . so she could still col-
> laborate with me on some things. It was funny, because with
> Claudia, competition was obvious. People would bring it up.
> With Lisa, it was much more silent. I guess I felt she needed to
> do a little bit more on her own. I think she was really wanting to
> take charge and didn't do it. I think there were times when she
> didn't want to disagree with me. And there got to be a point
> where she needed to, or she wanted to. It wasn't hard-core com-
> petition or anything.

Nancy's response strikes me on three levels. First, it is not altogether
clear how the anecdote she relates is an example of competitive feelings in the relationship. That very fact highlights her discomfort in
explicitly pointing out the area of competition. Second, she focuses
on Lisa's competitive feelings, as opposed to her own, once again indicating that competitive feelings in her friendships originate with
her friends. Third, it is one of several instances in which I feel an un-
derlying paternalism in her attitude toward Lisa. That is, she speaks
of Lisa almost in childlike terms in comparison to herself. In her descriptions of their relationship, Nancy often seems to be in a position
of dominance, helping Lisa out or making allowances for Lisa's diffi-

culties in navigating complex interpersonal situations. The very nature of Nancy's descriptions seem competitive. She is once again ahead of her friend.

Another example of this dynamic between Nancy and Lisa emerges when Nancy describes an incident involving Valerie, the supervisor who Nancy saw as first befriending her and later using Lisa against her. Nancy explains that the organization where they all used to work was putting together a group to go to a conference to present a paper on a program that she had developed. Valerie decided to send Lisa instead of Nancy, which Nancy describes as "incredibly mean." Nancy says, "And I had Lisa do it. She wasn't going to do it, but she wanted to do it. And I think it was a piece of that competition thing." Again, it is not altogether clear to me how the "competition thing" plays in here, particularly because she describes Lisa as troubled by the whole situation. Apparently, however, Nancy feels that Valerie's actions both highlighted and exacerbated any competitive feelings that Lisa might have had. Nancy seems to feel she rose above all that by making Lisa go. Once again, there is a paternalistic tone to Nancy's words that places her in charge within their relationship: "I had Lisa do it."

However, Nancy then backtracks and describes a workplace in which Lisa would have no need to feel competitive because Nancy has allowed Lisa the "space and room for her to develop." She seems to be saying, thus, that the reason there were *no* feelings of competition at work was because "in some ways I made room for her . . . she could take on stuff of her own, and be in charge of stuff, as opposed to if I had worked it so that everything had to be completely under me. There was more than enough room for two."

I ask Nancy if anything has come up in this realm as a result of pursuing her doctorate. Nancy smiles when I say that, as if she has thought about this before and understands quite well why that would not be an issue. She goes on to say:

> No, Lisa's not particularly academic. Even when we've presented, there have been times when, honestly, I've felt like, in an equal presentation, I've carried more of the weight. But it's a compromise you needed to make. She likes to learn, but she's never going to get her PhD, at least at this point in her life. She wants to present, and she likes to collaborate, to write, but to sit down by herself and do it is not something that she'd want to do.

Nancy seems to feel she has worked hard to try to prevent Lisa from feeling inferior to her and competitive with her. She has done so, in her own mind, by trying to allow room for Lisa to develop in their field in her own right. Yet, the nature of their professional and social relationship seems to be such that there is an inherent inequality that finds Nancy in a continuous position of superiority or dominance.

LINDA

> If a friend has to say they're better than you, or show they're better than you, or act like they're better than you, if that's between two women, then to me that's not a friendship. They can't be competitive and have a friendship.

Linda mentions competition at several points during the interview. However, like Nancy, she acknowledges it as an aspect of others' personalities, but not of her own. It is important to Linda that she not feel competitive with her friends and that, as a result, her friends do not need to feel competitive with her. Thus, when she mentions competition, it is to point out the lack of its existence in her best friendships.

Linda speaks of competition when she is comparing Emily's and her friendship with another of Emily's female friendships. Her description strikes me as multilayered in what it reveals about competitive feelings in the friendship:

> I think maybe what helps our relationship, and she's said this also, is that it's not a day-to-day thing. Because that puts a lot of stress on the friendship. Our kids never competed because we lived in different communities. She has a friend that lives across the street from her who she's very good friends with. This woman really adores Em, but she has a girl the same age as Em's daughter and that causes trouble.

Linda's comparison of the various children's relationships is embedded within a comparison of *her* friendship with Emily versus Emily's friendship with this other woman. According to Linda, she and Emily are able to have a friendship with far fewer difficulties (i.e., feelings of competition) than is the case for Emily and her neighbor. It is striking, as well, that Linda says that "this woman really adores

Em," without mentioning any reciprocity of feeling on Emily's part. It would have seemed more logical in the context of the story to tell of Emily's positive feelings toward her other friend, instead of the reverse. That she does not do so leads me to wonder if she has some difficulty acknowledging that the feelings may indeed be mutual.

Linda again brings up her own lack of feelings of competition while describing Emily's relationship with her older sister. When Linda tells me about the time several years ago when Emily revealed to her that her marriage was not what she had always led Linda to believe, she speculates that one of the reasons Emily did not discuss it with her was that she was talking to her sister about it and only needed to talk to one person. She goes on to say: "But I never felt in competition with her, because I knew Em was very close to her . . . and I think she viewed me much as I viewed my sister." That Linda brings up the potential for feeling competitive without any probing from me may well indicate that she does, indeed, experience some competitive feelings in this triangle. It seems important to her to make clear to me that Emily feels as close to her as to her sister—that in fact, as Linda repeats on other occasions, Emily views Linda very much like a sister, a relationship Linda clearly values for the closeness it implies.

It is evident both that competition and close friendship are, for Linda, mutually exclusive and that Linda is uncomfortable with the idea that she might feel competitive. Linda's discomfort in exploring, let alone acknowledging, the role of competition in her friendship with Emily comes through in her difficulty in articulating her thoughts:

> If someone is insensitive or if it's just a competing-type thing, then I don't pursue the friendship, because that's not who I am. And that's not who Em is. Some people, I don't know, something—I've never heard this, but I think, from what I've seen— this is another thing too, that we, we never really did compete, because we didn't go in the same social circle.

This idea of competing on a social level is something Linda brings up a few times. It seems to her to be the norm in the area in which she lives but something she does not consider herself to engage in. Its absence in her relationship with Emily is a sign for Linda of the strength of their friendship, compared with Emily's other friendships. According to Linda, by not being competitive, she provides a refuge for

Emily—a place to go where Emily's competitive tendencies can be put to rest. Interestingly, however, Linda then backtracks a bit, explaining that she does not think that Emily is actually competitive:

> I guess I always saw her as being kind of spoiled in that her husband had money, as did mine, so it wasn't that I was denied. But anything new that came out, she had to have it right away. She was the first to have anything, and if there was a place to go on vacation, she was the first one to go. In a sense, though, she just did it because that brought her pleasure. I don't know, maybe I'm rationalizing. But I don't think she did it—well, I don't know, I don't know why she did it, but I was going to say that she didn't do it to compete with other people. That that's just the way she is, which is different than the way I am, I think.

It is a testament to the distaste with which Linda regards competitive impulses that it is easier for her to think of Emily as spoiled ("maybe I'm rationalizing") than to think that Emily might be competitive.

When I ask Linda point blank what part, if any, she thinks competition plays in either of her two best friendships, her answer is quite long. She tells me that she has wondered how she fits into each of her two friends' groups of other friends, in terms of socioeconomic status. She notices that Carol has many friends who are wealthier than she, while Emily is the most well-off of her friends: "Where do I fit? I've imagined how I fit into their social structures. And I've wondered how they view me, more so than how I view them." Thus, she seems to be saying that she does not think about where they fit into *her* social structure, but she wonders how they consider her to fit into theirs. Again, that leaves others as the ones who are thinking in competitive terms. She then says, "Because in a way, we're all kind of financially the same, Carol and I and Em. So it's interesting for me to see who their other friends are. I'm not competitive and show-offish, so they're not with me."

Linda compares Carol and Emily to some extent, believing Emily to be more competitive. Yet she continues to waffle on this issue, sometimes saying Emily is competitive in other friendships, and other times claiming she is not and does not like people who are. Linda's difficulty in grappling with this issue is obvious. Her discomfort with the thought of competition entering her friendships is palpable. In fact, she explains toward the end of the second interview that she "would be hesitant to be friends with people professionally" because she would be concerned about the competitiveness that goes hand in hand with business relationships: "When competition is involved, the alarms go off." She then goes on to say that she would not necessarily consider it a problem to be applying for the same job as a person whom she liked in her academic program. If, however, the person "started doing things to promote herself, then, of course, I wouldn't like her." Thus, at the hint that competitive feelings could enter the picture, Linda would likely shut the door.

LIZ

> I think that women tend to be very competitive with one another. So it's very, very difficult to have a friendship if you have the same interests professionally, or if you have the same interests in terms of a mate or something like that.

Liz has thought a great deal about the role competition plays in female friendship. She believes that women are brought up to be competitive with one another and that, as a result, it is very difficult for them to be friends. She thinks that when women have similar interests and are at similar life-stages, it is virtually impossible to forge or to maintain a very close friendship, because of the competition that will emerge. She is particularly struck by how a mutual interest in a man can disrupt a friendship, even when the interest occurs years apart or is not that intense:

> In college, Susan and I had a good friend named Fran. We were all very, very good friends, and all of a sudden the friendship really kind of turned upside-down when Susan started dating an old boyfriend of Fran's. And Fran had only gone on about three dates with this guy, two years before. So it wasn't like it was this serious love of hers. But all of a sudden this intense competitiveness came in, and the words that were exchanged in very subtle overtones were very biting and in some ways very, very competitive. And their relationship became very, very strained, even though Susan went out with this guy maybe twice.

A similar thing happened to Liz when she believed that a friend of hers started to feel competitive after going out with Paul, a close friend, whom Liz had also briefly dated. The friendship between the women could not be sustained, yet Paul and Liz remained close.

Liz also talks about how similar professional interests can destroy a friendship. She describes a friendship she has with a woman with whom she used to work that was sustained only because they did not have the same ambitions. According to Liz, when she applied for a job that eventually turned her into Mary's boss, there were no difficulties. The situation could have been different, however:

> But I think if she had wanted that job, or if I knew she was applying and because of that I didn't apply because I was worried about the friendship, I don't think that friendship could have lasted. I really don't. And we're still very, very good friends. But I do think it's difficult when you have the same interests, in terms of profession, or men, or whatever. I think it can cause a huge conflict. No matter how meaningless the guy is to you or how much you say that the job doesn't matter to you, I think it can be a really serious problem.

Although Liz talks about competition in friendship in very different terms than does Linda, their ultimate conclusion is similar—close female friendship cannot be sustained in the face of competition. It is important to note that Liz does not think that she has found a way to have two very close friendships *despite* competitive feelings. Rather, these friendships have formed and survived because there is no basis for competition:

L: I just think it's interesting that the women that are by far the closest to me are women that if you saw us standing on the street you wouldn't necessarily put together. I mean, just standing there you wouldn't necessarily say, "Oh, those two are friends."

P: I know you said that you and Susan dress very differently.

L: Yeah. And Sandy, you might put Sandy and me together, but certainly if you wrote up what we did, just gave us a biography of age, what we did, what we studied in college, who our spouses are, I don't think you'd put any of us together.

In other words, Liz and her friends have been able to maintain their friendships because they have nothing to compete about.

Finally, Liz, like Linda and Nancy, does not want to see herself as competitive: "I don't think of myself as being a competitive person, and I certainly don't like to be competitive." However, a short time later Liz tells me about a female friend from high school who became competitive with her because she wanted to go to college where Liz went, but was not admitted. I then ask Liz, "But you think that comes from her, not from you?" Liz replies:

> I'm sure I play a part in it. I mean I can honestly tell you that I must play a part in it, because I feel like this is a constant thing I encounter, so it must come from me in part.

Thus, she seems open to the possibility that she may have a part in the competitive dynamic. But she then goes on:

> I drive myself incredibly hard and maybe that can be perceived as competitive, although I never really feel the need to compare myself to anyone. I mean I would never ask someone, "What did you get on this paper?" because I don't care. What I really care about is where I'm at and what my level is, but maybe that's perceived as competitive.

So, in fact, Liz believes only that she might be perceived as being competitive, not that she, herself, would harbor such feelings.

REFLECTIONS

Ask a woman you know how she feels about competitiveness or if she, herself, is competitive, and you are likely to feel seasick watching her navigate through and articulate her attitudes and beliefs about the subject. As is evident with Nancy, Linda, and Liz, few women find it easy to deal with, understand, or describe how competitiveness fits into their lives and relationships. All three women have thought about competition as an issue that can affect friendships. Linda and Liz see competition as a wholly destructive force. For Linda, it is destructive because she cannot tolerate it. If she believes it exists, she will likely abandon the friendship. Liz is saying something only slightly different: Competition between women is difficult to avoid, but the only way to have a close friendship is to avoid it. Thus, they both can see that competition exists in other relationships, but feel it has no place in their closest friendships. Nancy, in contrast, acknowledges that competitive feelings have found their way into both of her friendships. But she does not seem all that comfortable with those feelings as part of the friendship dynamic and has at times worked to prevent their emergence. What is most striking for me is the discomfort that all three women have with any sign that the competitive feelings might emanate from within themselves. Clearly, having competitive feelings toward one's friends is perceived as an enormous negative. Thus, at the least suggestion that perhaps they, themselves, might feel competitive at times, all three women backtrack.

There is a relatively large amount of literature on women and competition that is helpful in understanding the discomfort women feel about these issues. Studies have noted that women and men seem to react differently to competition, given a range of situations under which the competition takes place.[1] Many indicate that men perform better under competitive circumstances than do women. Researchers such as Lever, Horner, and Sassen have tried to understand the roots of this gender difference.[2]

Lever, considering "the peer group as the *agent* of socialization," studied boys and girls at play.[3] She believed that through understanding the differences in the way the two gender groups play as children, we might better understand how they come to be equipped with different skills as adults. She found, among other things, that boys' games last longer than girls' games, in part because boys "resolve their disputes more effectively."[4] For Lever, that meant that while the boys argued frequently during games, they always came up with resolutions and the games continued. The girls, in contrast, often terminated their games in the face of disputes. Lever also found that whereas the boys' games invariably involved direct competition, the nature of the competition in girls' games was usually indirect. For example, in games such as jump rope there are no clear winners or losers. At most, achievements are compared. In addition, girls were far more likely than boys to play without overtly competing. For example, girls often played pretend games in which they took on the roles of relationships. Similarly, whereas girls may have chosen to simply ride their bikes together, boys were more likely to decide to race one another down the street. Lever also found that girls liked to play in dyads and small groups, whereas boys tended to play in large groups.

Lever believed that boys' experiences with play prepares them for the marketplace, while girls' experiences prepare them for the private sphere—that is, for roles as wives and mothers. She claimed that girls do not learn to negotiate rules the way boys do and therefore "gain little experience in the judicial process."[5] Essentially, boys learn to compete:

> A boy and his best friend often find themselves on opposing teams. They must learn ways to resolve disputes so that the quarrels do not become so heated that they rupture friendships. Boys must learn to "depersonalize the attack." Not only do they learn to compete against friends, they also learn to cooperate with teammates whom they may or may not like personally.[6]

As adults, men are thus better equipped to be openly and forthrightly competitive.

Certainly, my findings bear out Lever's contention that women have not learned to compete "in a forthright manner."[7] All three women seem to feel competitive at times, but none acknowledges engaging in outright competition with her closest friends. This is perhaps most evident with Nancy, who describes specific events in which she was competing, even as she tells me that she never perceived the situations as competitive. This lack of acknowledgment seems to result, in the case of her friendship with Lisa, in a repeated pattern of behavior that may well make Lisa feel inferior. It is unlikely, based on Nancy's expressions of her feelings for Lisa, that she would consciously choose to make her friend feel that way.

Other theorists have tried to come to understand how women conceptualize competitive situations.[8] A significant development in the work on women's feelings about competition came about when Horner developed her theory of "fear of success."[9] Horner believed that to understand women's apparent lack of achievement motivation, one had to understand what success meant to women. Through her work, Horner came to believe that many women feared success because they felt that success and femininity were not compatible. She said that women feared that with success would come "social rejection" and a "loss of femininity." Thus, competition leads to a feeling of anxiety for women because of its possible outcome. Horner found, however, that women who experience fear of success seem only to do so in competitive circumstances. That is, women in her studies achieved as expected when the goal put before them was just to do as well as they could. Their achievement levels were suppressed only when they were competing against others.

Horner's theories came out of her belief that women during the early 1970s were afraid of being viewed as less feminine in the eyes of men. Although that belief may have little bearing on the current study, it could be argued that Nancy, Liz, and Linda do in some way fear a diminished sense of femininity, given a very different set of parameters for that word than Horner used. That is, for these three women, their definition of femininity may include their sense of themselves as friends to other women, something that could be seen as compromised by engaging in competition. This idea should become clearer in light of the work of Sassen.

Although much work was done on fear of success following Horner's study, more recent work has focused on whether Horner's conception of fear of success is indeed at work in women's apparent inner conflict regarding competition. Sassen approached the question of women's feelings about competition somewhat differently from Horner. She pointed out that Horner defined anxiety as occurring when an individual expects that there will be negative consequences to his or her actions. Sassen explained that Robert Kegan provided another definition. According to Sassen, Kegan described the experience of anxiety "as the sense of disintegration which occurs when a meaning-making organism finds itself unable to make meaning."[10] In applying this definition to Horner's findings, Sassen wrote: "[T]he women in Horner's . . . samples are not simply afraid [of succeeding]. They are unable to take competitive success and construct around it a vision, a new way of making sense, to which they can feel personally committed."[11] To further explain her point of view, Sassen brought in the relational theories of Chodorow and Gilligan, both of whom have emphasized that throughout their lives girls are taught to value relationships.[12] The goal of winning in competition, Sassen believed, is in direct contradiction to what women have come to value—that is, the preservation and fostering of relationships. The anxiety many women feel in competition is a result of the relationship meaning-making they bring to such situations: "Women bring a relational, contextual structure of knowing to the cue they are asked to make sense of, and thus find they cannot accommodate it to this kind of competitive success."[13]

Sassen further explained that women see another side of success achieved through competition—that is, the emotional costs. It is this other side that I alluded to previously in discussing Horner's conclusions about women's fearing a loss of femininity in the face of succeeding through competition. If women greatly value the connectedness of relationships, as Chodorow, Gilligan, and others have pointed out, it seems natural that competition would cause them some anxiety.[14] If one is trying to be *the* winner, someone else is going to be the loser. It feels, at best, difficult to remain connected in the way that women are used to when one is pursuing such an individualist goal. Further, women are judged and judge themselves according to their ability to care for others. Trying to beat one's opponent could feel very much anathema to that ethic of care.[15] As Sassen said, it would be very difficult to make sense of this type of competition using a parameter of meaning-making that values connectedness and caring.

Similarly, Johannessen pointed out that the resulting conflict can lead to "competitive anxiety," which in turn can lead to feelings of vulnerability. She saw the process of competing as inherently dichotomous in that one is necessarily both separating from and relating to another, causing a great deal of dissonance. Anxiety develops as the woman contends with a coexisting desire to succeed and a fear of the impact that success will have on the relationship. The woman's vulnerability, in turn, results from considering what she has to lose (the relationship) should she engage in competition with her friends.[16]

Thus, as competitive feelings begin to arise, women have reason for discomfort. Lever believed that men, unlike women, can comfortably compete as adults because they understand how to "depersonalize the attack," thereby enabling them to effectively combine friendship and competition.[17] But, as Sassen and the relational theorists have pointed out, the meanings women make of female friendship and of competition do not seem to accommodate one another.[18] Thus, Nancy, Linda, and Liz have apparently not found a way to reconcile their conceptions of themselves as good, caring friends with the competitive feelings that almost seem to force their way to the surface despite the women's best efforts to suppress them.

More recent researchers and theorists have explored the possibility of finding a way to construct a model for competition that is more compatible with women's ways of relating. In her dissertation, Ford wrote about Lindenbaum's thoughts regarding the connection between envy and competition.[19] According to Ford, Lindenbaum, in her work with lesbian couples, came to believe that envy and competition can be placed at differing points on a spectrum of healthy ways of relating to others, with envy often signaling a more unhealthy manner of relating. Lindenbaum found that among many of the lesbian couples who came into her practice, envy resulted from the women's desire to become merged with their partners. She believed that, in general, along with this desire, comes the wish to gain the attributes of the partner, as well as an unconscious feeling of envy that the other's ownership of those attributes necessarily deprives one's self of such ownership.

Lindenbaum claimed that the envy leads to a competitive inhibition, because women usually see envy and competition as inextricably intertwined. Since they strive to avoid both their own and the other's envy for fear of the consequent loss of merger, they also avoid competition. She suggested, however, that competition can be healthy in women's relationships with other women, because when engaged in overtly, competition can allow the women to see that attributes do not have to be gained at the expense of the other person. That is, there is enough of an attribute to go around. Lindenbaum further went on to say that competition could even motivate women to strive for higher goals as they work together as individuals, without fearing that the relationship will be damaged by their separateness. In other words, she believed that a woman can compete within a relatedness construct and ultimately view the other's success as inspiring to her own endeavors.

Miner, in writing about competition among feminist writers, also proposed an alternative construct for competition.[20] She believed, as did Ford, Lindenbaum, and Johannessen, that competition as it is currently formulated in the culture is "masculinist." She wrote: "I have found a need to distinguish between competition for ego gratification within the androcentric system, i.e., fame and status, and competition for our own standards of aesthetic excellence."[21] She called for a "cooperative competition" in which women's relationist styles would be put to use.[22] She believed that women writers could work in groups together, helping each other, even with an awareness that the publishing world is such that if one manuscript is published, another might not be. She realized that there would be jealousies and arguments, but believed that by working together each individual would be stimulated to stretch her own abilities.

Similarly, Meyer-Pfaff talked about a Competition and Cooperation Model, in which women maintain the connectedness they so value as they work to attain their goals. She believed that most women do not want to be "number one," because in attaining that position they may harm others. Rather, through the motivation and support they get in their relationships, women feel most comfortable striving to "realize their full self-potential."[23] As women attain success, increases in self-esteem will result, which will lead to an ability to "empower others." Finally, as women work together, relationships among them will develop and strengthen.

A distinction must be made between learning how to compete with other women without becoming anxious or allowing the friendship to disintegrate and learning how to accept the competitive feelings that most human beings seem to feel. Liz believes that girls are raised to be competitive with each other from an early age and boys are not. Lever believed that boys are taught how to compete and girls are not. These are clearly two different phenomena. Lever is talking about direct and sanctioned competition—at that age, games. But Liz is referring to social competition, for friends and for boys. It is this competitiveness that seems to make most women, particularly those with a feminist orientation, most uncomfortable. We feel that we simply should not experience the impulse of wanting to be more successful than our friends. Linda, Liz, and Nancy, all through differing means, strive to set up their relationships with their closest friends so that competitive feelings cannot seep in. I think each wants to believe she accomplished her goal because there is nothing that she recognizes as a source of competitive feelings. Yet, although none wants a relationship in which there is an obvious reason to compete, it might well be easier for them to accept their own competitive feelings if they *were* in direct competition with their friends. As it is, their competitive feelings are taboo. They are taboo, in all likelihood, because to feel competitive with a friend feels anathema to close female friendship. How can we care for a friend and simultaneously compare ourselves to our friends, hoping to come out just slightly ahead—or as Meyer-Pfaff might suggest, at least on a par? It seems incompatible with the values we believe should be inherent in close relationships.

It is in this realm that Lindenbaum's suggestions seem most useful. Envy and competitiveness do indeed seem related—and envy never feels good, because it comes from a feeling of inferiority. But if, as Lindenbaum says, we can transform envy into a healthy competitiveness, we may better be able to see that the success of our friend does not diminish our own accomplishments, and vice versa.

Direct competition between women is a different story, and perhaps Lever is right that if we had all been competing on the playing field at a young age we would not find it so difficult to do so as adults. But there is also that other sticking point that someone is trying to be the winner—and trying to make someone else (a friend) the loser— that just does not sit right with many women. Although the models presented earlier are useful in theory, implementing them is quite another story. But certainly it seems likely that the best advice female friends in competition could receive is to keep the lines of communication open. Studies have shown the importance of talk in female friendships. Talking is how women stay connected. Thus, although it is unlikely that the discomfort involved in competing with a close friend could be eliminated, perhaps some of the fears of the dissolution of the friendship could be diminished with communication.

Finally, it is important to note that girls today are involved on a greater scale in athletic competition than they were when Lever wrote her article in 1976 and when most of my participants were young. That serves both to expose them to competition at a young age and, one would imagine, to foster a culture in which competitive impulses among women are more acceptable than when I was struggling to balance my simultaneous desire to beat my opponent with my wish to preserve our relationship.

Chapter 6

Alice

Alice is a thirty-six-year-old single white woman, living alone in a one-bedroom apartment. She has a master's degree, and was doing freelance work at the time of the interviews. We conducted both interviews at her kitchen table.

My first interview with Alice was the longest of all my interviews, and I ended it only because we both seemed to have run out of steam. However, I wanted to ask her more even before I had had a chance to review the transcript, and it was clear to me that she had more to say. In fact, after I turned off the tape recorder, she asked me if she would have a chance to talk about any of her other close female friendships.

I found Alice's narrative to be extremely engrossing. On a few occasions, I even asked her questions that were not particularly germane to my research, but that were of interest to me in the context of the story. It was not until later, however, while I was transcribing the interview, and again when I reviewed the transcript, that I was struck that in telling the story of her friendship with Julia, Alice essentially told Julia's story. She told me very little about herself, particularly, during that first interview.

THE STORY

Alice's apparent reticence in talking about herself does not reflect a general style in talking about her friendship. She is extraordinarily forthcoming about what she sees as the problems in the friendship. She has clearly put a great deal of thought into the difficulties in communicating that she perceives to exist between Julia and herself and expresses concern about what they will mean for the long-term health of the friendship:

Julia and I met in the fifth grade. My family had just moved to Adelston, and she had lived there since probably the second grade. We weren't in the same class, but we had a mutual friend who was in my class. We became kind of a threesome, although they were closer. And then in sixth grade, Julia and I were in the same class and we became very good friends. We just kind of hit it off. Our senses of humor really clicked. Neither of us were particularly popular kids. We sort of liked to consider ourselves as somewhat on the fringe. And we were very creative. We were both really into writing, so we would sometimes do projects together. She was a great student and she always got a lot of attention from the teachers. I think I sort of emulated that in a way and looked up to her for that.

But our friendship really kind of got off to a slow start for a whole variety of reasons. She had a lot of problems at home. She had very repressive parents and a very critical, repressive father. She was very, very secretive about her home life, and didn't really want to have people over, including me. And it sort of caused some uncertainty on my part, although I was feeling very close to her. It took awhile for me to figure out that it wasn't that she didn't like me. I had a lot of insecurities about the friendship, because at times I felt like, "Gee, she really likes me but she won't invite me over to her house, so maybe that means she doesn't really like me as much as I thought she did." But then in junior high and high school, those times when I did go over there, I began to understand that there was a real tension in that house. Her father—he's passed away—was just this very big guy, who kind of ruled the roost. He was domineering and very critical. It just didn't feel like a house where kids were too accepted in all their facets. So it was probably as much what I discerned from being there as it was what she said, because she didn't say much.

Alice continues with Julia's story:

Julia actually ended up marrying one of her high school teachers. I think she got involved with him while we were still in school. At some point she told me that they were starting to get more . . . well to become friends really. But more than friends, and I wasn't sure what she meant. But I didn't really push her very much about it. I didn't like the man. In fact, I couldn't stand him. He was a very charismatic teacher, but not a good guy. And he had married a student before, so it was a pattern of his. I think Julia really cared about him, but I think she also really wanted to get out of her house. That's my assessment of it, but I think she would agree with that.

I saw the relationship growing, and they started spending more time together, but she was pretty secretive about it, about what was really going on. I didn't really probe very much because I was a little—I guess this is one aspect of the friendship—there are often times when I worry about her, but I don't really express it, because I guess my philosophy is that I feel like people kind of find their own way. I feel like I need to trust my friends to find their own way, and sometimes I feel like my concern turns into pushiness.

But I had a party at my house before we graduated, and she invited him over. And I got into a really big argument with him. He was a very argumentative, sullen type of man. Sometimes downright mean. And I felt like I was trying to hold myself back from saying anything to Julia, but I think it was probably obvious to her that I didn't like him. I think there was a point when I finally said to her that I really didn't care for him. She kind of probed me about it at a certain point before she went to college, in a kind of joking way, like, "I don't think you like Mike very much." And I said, "Yeah, you're right. I'm not sure he's such a good person for you. He's a lot older. Do you really think you want to be with him?"

During the years that Julia was with Mike, Alice felt increasingly isolated from her friend:

So then she went to college and we had a lot of periods of, I guess, distance— geographical distance, and also some emotional distances. When she went to college, we wrote to each other and we were in touch by phone, and she visited me at college, but that was more after she left college and lived in Clarkstown and lived with him. But we kind of grew apart just a little bit. And then the years that she was with this man, with her husband, she was very out of touch with me. I had such mixed feelings. I suppose I feel like I pulled back too, because it was very hard. She kind of wound up in a situation where she was with a man who was very much like her father, very repressive. He really didn't allow her any free-dom. Being allowed to come see me at school was a big deal for her. So we had a big gap. There was kind of a big gap between the time we were both nineteen and then maybe, gosh, it really was long, maybe nineteen and twenty-four, when she started emerging from the marriage. She went into counseling and she got out of the marriage at twenty-five. So during that period, there were a lot of things I didn't know about what was happening with her. She tried to keep in touch with me, but I didn't feel she was very accessible at all. In fact, quite the opposite. It wasn't that I thought she didn't care for me, but I felt that she kind of had seques-tered herself in this marriage. And I didn't want to burden her in a certain way, too. Looking back on it, I feel kind of bad that I didn't get more involved because I think that she really needed contact, she needed my friendship, but I wasn't sure how to be there because I felt shut out. And I almost felt like the best suggestion I could make was for her to leave this man, which didn't feel totally appropriate.

As Alice reflects on those years when they were not in touch, she sees aspects of the friendship still present that made it difficult for her to reach out to Julia back then:

But I do have a lot of regrets. We were such close friends, and maybe I didn't try hard enough to find out what was going on with her. Maybe it's a personality thing between us, but I find it's hard sometimes to know how to find out what's really happening for her as opposed to what's on the surface. And usually my tendency has been to let her come forth, because I've always felt she doesn't re-ally like to be pushed on things. Even now I don't like to push her. Or to confront her about things. Recently, I did have occasion to, though. She lives in Vermont now and I see her only occasionally. But she was down for the holidays. And she was very busy. When she comes down, she has to do family things because Larry—her second husband—has a big family, and she just is running around here seeing people. But a couple of times when she's come down here, she has-n't stopped by, and I'm not really out of the way at all. It kind of surprised me. I felt hurt that she didn't make time just to even stop in for an hour or something, since we get to see each other so rarely. And I know I tend to be a little sensitive to things like that, but I felt hurt. So I wrote her, because I didn't feel comfortable saying it. This is another facet of our relationship, or at least for me in our relationship. I just worry about being too demanding as a friend, and I think this really goes back to our childhood, because I was very aware of Julia having demands on her. Like at home, and then in her marriage. They occupied a lot of energy and stuff, and I just worried about being too demanding. And I think I still do. So even to say something about this situation was kind of a big deal. To say that I was sad. I didn't even feel comfortable saying it to her. I felt like I had to write it, which is a little wimpy.

But she called me after she got the letter and she was very, very apologetic. In fact, this was one of those situations where it was almost like I felt like she didn't have to be apologizing that much, because I wasn't trying to make her feel guilty. I just wanted to bring it up and maybe tell her that I was feeling bad about it. But she felt really guilty.

Although Alice clearly feels very close to Julia, it becomes increasingly evident that there are areas of the friendship that frustrate her and that she would like to change—if only she knew how:

It's funny, we have a friendship in which there's a lot of love and support, and a lot of history and a lot of commonality in our interests, in our lives, and in our values, but a lot of things aren't said. There are a lot of, not necessarily secrets, but things that aren't spoken. It is very hard for me to introduce conflicts with Julia. Conflicts often get side-stepped. There's a lack of that sort of open expression of quote-unquote negative feelings or displeasure, or disagreement in our friendship. That's probably true of some other close friends of mine, too, but not all. It's almost a little easier for me with male friends to introduce a conflict. I don't know why. It's an old pattern with Julia. It's a way we relate. But I'm not happy with it, because I feel it really stops our friendship from growing. It's kind of like cutting off a part of the friendship or a part of who I am. And I wonder how much that's true for her, too.

One thing that's sort of an issue for me now is Julia's weight. It's really changed a lot. She's gone from being pretty slim to being really overweight. And she and her husband have been talking about having children, or having a child, and I've been really concerned about her health. Just because when women are heavy they *can* carry babies, but it's not so great. Or even just as a habit, a lifelong health concern. It's been a situation where I'd like to be supportive in the right way. But I've had a lot of issues around food myself. I was borderline anorexic for awhile when I was in college. And it's very hard for me to confront that issue. So it's a concern, but it's something that's really hard to know how to bring up constructively. Another part of it is that it's easier to look at someone else's life and point out what's not working than it is to face what's not working in our own lives. But lately I've been thinking about bringing it up.

As is echoed throughout many of the participants' stories, Alice is also frustrated by Julia's reluctance to reach out to her in times of need. (See Chapter 8 for an in-depth discussion of feelings of dependence and independence in best friendships.)

Another thing about our friendship is that when she's going through difficult times, when stuff starts coming up for her, she'll be out of touch. She won't call or write. She'll kind of drop out of the picture a little bit while she's sorting things out. And when I've asked her about it, she says that she's worried that she's going to become a burden. That her kind of talking about these problems or what's bothering her is going to become a real burden, and that I'm going to get sick of it, or sick of her. So this has been going on for a long, long time—for years—and she's very quick to want to be of help to me, but it almost seems like she's not comfortable asking for help or talking about what's on her mind. And I tell her, "You're not a burden. You're my oldest friend and dearest friend in the world, and I want to know what's going on with you. I want to hear everything." I feel really sad about it, but I also understand it, because I think I'm that way a little bit too. I'm very conscious of not wanting to be too dependent. I have this thing about not wanting to add to people's problems.

And yet, there are difficult issues that Alice and Julia do find a way to discuss, even if at times Alice is not completely satisfied with the outcome. We sense, however, that she will keep trying:

She also doesn't raise conflicts with me, although she'll kind of point things out to me when she feels strongly about them. For instance, I was dating a guy last year who she really disliked, and in a very tactful way she told me she didn't think he was any good for me. And I really trust her. I mean at first I was kind of pissed. I still liked the guy and didn't want to see what she was seeing. But there was something in the back of my mind that really wanted her opinion and really wanted to hear what she felt. I guess that was why I introduced them. She was the only friend who had met him. I guess I really trust her instinct. And I was having a little trouble knowing what was right. There were these issues that were coming up for me with him. So ultimately I was grateful. And she's coming down this weekend and will meet my boyfriend, Andy. I'll definitely ask her what she thinks of him. I mean if I'm totally off-base, she probably will wait for me to ask her. But otherwise, she'll probably just say, "Oh, I think he's wonderful." She's kind of hesitant to speak when she knows it's not particularly positive, but she will. It's just she wants to make sure I want to hear it. But it's really important to me what she thinks. If she had some really strong negative feelings about Andy, I would really listen, and I would take that into account.

Another thing that's been kind of an issue between us, which we have discussed, is money issues. Like recently, I told her that what I wanted for my birthday was to take her to a retreat. I really wanted to go with her, and I knew that with her financial circumstances it would be hard for her. So I wanted to take her. And eventually she agreed, which was kind of an amazing thing because she has a lot of pride about being able to pay for herself all the time. We get into conflicts over who's going to pay for dinner. For instance, if I go up to visit her, I'll want to take her out, or maybe for her birthday I'll want to pay for dinner, and she won't let me. So with this retreat, she agreed but then kind of went back on her word. When we got there and we were together, she said, "Thank you for paying for this, but I really feel I have to pay for it." So what I saw as a present for her and for myself, it turns out she wants to pay me back. And I can understand that, but I was really kind of frustrated. And maybe a little bit angry. It feels like such a control issue or something, but I just don't fully have a grasp on it. So we've talked about it some, but it does come up over and over again.

We've also talked about her marriage to Mike, her first husband. After she got out of the marriage, we started seeing each other again. I started going over to her apartment fairly frequently. She was much more forthcoming than before about what had happened and about what she was feeling. I felt more able to approach her and to talk to her about what had been going on. I mean she still didn't say a lot, and I still didn't probe a lot, but things came out. It was really painful for her to talk about it. And I've told her some of what I felt during that period. I've told her about feeling very cut off and that I didn't want to confront her with my concerns. So I feel like a lot of that is resolved. But at the same time, there's a part there that isn't. I guess I still have some pretty strong emotions about what was going on for her—and what was going on for me, which was basically that I felt like my best friend had disappeared into a black hole. It was very hard. And part of it that I haven't really fully expressed to her is that I feel a lot of guilt about that. That I wasn't there. I feel like I could have done more. That maybe I could have helped her get out of the marriage. Or at least been there to hear what was really going on for her, which at the time I had no idea how to ask her.

I know I was young at the time, and I think if I saw her getting into a situation like that again it would be clearer to me what was happening. I think I would say something if I thought she was in trouble. But part of the problem is that it's a very touchy thing to get involved with a friend's marriage. But again, where it relates to her feelings about herself and her self-esteem, I feel that I could stand to learn how to be more up-front with her, more honest. For instance, I don't know how much the weight problem is related to things in her marriage, but I feel like there is some connection. She started getting heavier about a year into the marriage. So I feel like it's related in some way to her relationship with her husband. And it's something I've wanted to broach with her and I feel like I'm sort of getting closer to doing that, but it feels very difficult to do that on the phone. It feels very difficult to do it period. But I feel like if I'm not going to talk to her about it, nobody will. But I also feel a lot of hesitation about doing it. I don't want her to think I don't like Larry. I do.

Finally, Alice conveys, in few words, how important Julia is to her and why, despite the difficulties between them, Julia is her best friend:

Julia is incredibly kind and incredibly warm, loving, and supportive as a friend. She's very, very attentive. I hope I'm as attentive as she is of me. I hope she feels I am. She really is aware of what's going on in my life, on a pretty consistent basis. She expresses concern and interest in what I'm doing. She's sensitive and she hears how I'm feeling even if I'm not saying it. She has a very light-hearted side to her. She has a really good sense of humor. Sometimes a really wicked sense of humor. We've always connected in that way pretty strongly, ever since we knew each other as kids. She has a very positive, hopeful outlook. She's a very nurturing friend. She'll send me notes or supportive little e-mails. We e-mail each other a fair bit. If I'm going through a hard time, she'll send me e-mails or notes. So she's very warm, but there's not a lot of physical touching or anything. It's more through talking.

Having her in my life since we were kids gives the friendship a real continuity for me. We have a history together. And that feels really important. Sometimes I feel like she's my superego. I have a sense that she kind of looks after me, in a way that is a little bit almost like a conscience. And I feel that there's a mutual support. Despite the breaks in contact, I still feel there's a supportive thread that's run through the whole friendship. Being able to talk to somebody who I know knows me for a long time and through a lot of different changes is important to me. And maybe things aren't always as honest as I'd like them to be, but she knows me and there is still a lot of honesty there.

FURTHER REFLECTIONS:
COMMUNICATION BREAKDOWNS

A thread that runs throughout Alice's story of her friendship with Julia is her concern about their communication difficulties and, consequently, the many things that have been left unsaid over their years of friendship. Alice is the only one of the participants to express, from the beginning of our interviews, uneasy feelings about her friendship. Although she cares for Julia deeply, and knows that Julia cares for her, she feels there are aspects of the friendship that could work better for her.

As Alice sees it, their difficulties in communication were established early in the friendship, when Alice sensed that Julia was unhappy at home but did not talk about it with Julia. My sense from Alice is that she believes Julia's father may have been emotionally and/or physically abusive. It was not, however, until I began writing about and looking for evidence for that, that I realized that Alice never uses those words to describe Julia's father. I remember feeling during the interview that Alice, in fact, dances around the words, perhaps never articulating her beliefs because Julia never verified them. That is, it may well be that Alice and Julia have never had a conversation in which Julia told Alice exactly what had been going on in her home. Interestingly, although I wondered during the interview if Alice does think that Julia's father was abusive, I never asked her. I may have received signals from Alice, just as she may have from Julia, that to further pursue this topic would be too great an invasion of privacy. Thus, the dynamic that Alice and I built up around this topic may be resonant of Julia and Alice's difficulties in communicating.

As Alice and Julia continued on to high school, another significant area of Julia's life became a topic that the two of them did not fully

discuss. Alice intimates that she had suspicions about the relationship
between Julia and their teacher, Mike, but she chose "not to probe
very much." She says that Julia was very secretive about it, but also
says that Julia hinted at the nature of the relationship:

> And at some point she told me that they were starting to get
> more . . . well to become friends, really. But kind of more than
> friends, and I wasn't sure what she meant, but I didn't really
> push her very much about it.

Alice recognizes that a dynamic of their relationship had already become set at that point:

> Well, I guess this is one aspect of the friendship, there are often
> times when I worry about her but I don't really express it . . . it's
> not that I don't express it, but I don't kind of push it too much.

Alice goes on to say that she prefers to let Julia "come forth," because
"I've always felt she doesn't really like to be pushed on things." But
when I ask her why she thinks that about Julia, she considers that it
may be a reflection of her own difficulty with confronting people
rather than anything Julia has said or done.

In any relationship, a dynamic develops from which it is impossible to tease out at what point aspects of the dynamic began. Although
Alice may indeed find it difficult to confront people, it may also well
be that she is taking cues from Julia. Certainly, Julia was secretive
about her family life and her developing relationship with Mike.
Then, after she and Mike got married, Julia did not share with Alice
all that was going on in her marriage. Yet Alice regrets that she did
not read the signs better and reach out to Julia rather than follow
Julia's lead in being silent about what was apparently going on. Although I think Alice is asking a lot of herself as a young woman facing the difficulties of growing up (e.g., she was dealing with her own
anorexia during a portion of this period), it is somewhat striking that
she apparently could not imagine a way to be a friend without telling
Julia that she should leave her husband. In hindsight, however, Alice
does indicate that perhaps she could have just provided friendship—
some contact.

There are also current examples of what Alice perceives as communication difficulties in her friendship with Julia. During the first

interview, she mentions that she has difficulty telling Julia when Julia has hurt her. She also says that she would like to talk to Julia about her concerns about Julia's weight gain and its possible relationship to her current marriage. Alice's internal struggle about not being able to discuss such issues of significance with Julia is palpable, particularly those that she sees as affecting Julia's happiness. She seems to long to be able to find a way to broach these subjects with Julia, yet there is no precedent in their friendship for doing so. She feels a responsibility to be open with Julia and push Julia to be open with her—not to make the mistake of silence she feels she has made in the past. But this is countered by a fear of what will result if she does so—perhaps it is a fear of the unknown.

By the second interview, Alice and Julia have talked about some of these issues. Alice has written Julia a letter about the hurt feelings she felt when Julia did not come to see her on a recent visit home, and Julia has called to apologize. In fact, Julia was so apologetic that Alice began to feel bad about making Julia feel guilty. Thus, although Alice seems to be glad she wrote the letter and aired her feelings, she does not feel altogether satisfied with the outcome.

The subjects of Julia's weight and her marriage were raised by Julia in the intervening time between the two interviews. Although that allowed Alice to say some of what was on her mind, she essentially let Julia take the lead as Alice took on a listening and supportive role. Thus, although Alice expresses to me that she is pleased that they talked, and that her concerns about talking about Julia's current marriage were not borne out, she has not yet found a way to take the initiative she describes wanting to take in broaching such topics.

Although Alice takes on a good share of the blame for the difficulties she perceives in her friendship with Julia, she also recognizes that in friendships she has formed as an adult, the lines of communication are often far more open. She very much wishes that she could find a way to change the pattern that was set in her friendship with Julia at such an early age:

> I guess we've sort of fallen into some patterns over time. One of them is about nonconfrontation. And I'm not very happy with it because I feel like it really stops our friendship from growing, in a way. It's kind of like cutting off a part of the friendship or cutting off who I am, and I wonder how much that's true for her too.

Alice seems to feel as if she is not fully realized in that relationship as the person she has grown into. Furthermore, because of the love and warmth she feels toward Julia, and the value she places on the relationship, she worries about the health and future of the friendship.

Chapter 7

Amy

Amy is a twenty-seven-year-old Asian-American, studying to get a doctorate. I interviewed Amy twice, both times in her apartment, which she shares with her husband. We sat at a small table at which they probably ate their meals. During the interviews, Amy laughed a lot—very often when talking about subjects about which I thought she might feel uncomfortable. I think her laughing in what I perceived to be a nervous way had the effect both of distancing me from what she was saying and of making me want, at times, to dig a little deeper to find out what was behind the laughter. Although there were times when I felt that I was just scratching the surface of what was going on for Amy, there were other times when I believed that she was really struggling to understand something for herself and to try to explain it to me.

An area of difficulty arose for me concerning Amy's intimation in our first interview that she had experienced some kind of sexual abuse. She brought this up by way of describing an area of commonality between her and her friend Janine, since Janine had also experienced some sort of trauma. After the interview, I felt unsure as to whether I should ask Amy more about these experiences. I thought it might be intrusive for me to do so, but I also wondered if by bringing it up, she wanted me to further pursue it. What I came to realize was that the answer lay in how the research would best be served. That is, would it be useful information for me to have? Ultimately, I decided that it would be, since it was clearly an important area of commonality for Amy and her friend. Thus, in the second interview I asked her about it but also emphasized that if she did not want to tell me she did not have to.

THE STORY

Janine

As Amy introduces us to Janine and to their friendship, we learn one of the most important facets about Amy's life—that she is a born-again Christian:

Janine and I met in college. We lived on the same floor during our freshman year. Our floor was an all-women's floor, so it was a nice environment for cultivating friendships. And although we didn't know each other well—during our freshman year we had separate peer groups—we knew of each other and definitely were in contact pretty frequently. We were both parts of different Christian organizations on campus, and so through that we also had additional contact. And, I'd say, sophomore year our friendship started to solidify a little bit more. But it was really in our junior year of college that we started to build a strong friendship. We were going to the same church at the time, and we lived in an apartment with Nina, my other friend, and two other women. Janine and I were roommates that year. So I'd say that was when we really solidified our friendship, because we were with each other so much and really got to share a lot of our lives with each other. And senior year we lived in adjacent apartments. So I saw a lot of her then, as well.

I was a bridesmaid in her wedding, and she was my maid of honor. And we've kept in touch since college, although it's been increasingly sporadic because of time constraints. But we still keep in touch frequently. And when I do see her—we make a point of trying to see each other every couple of months—it feels very much like not very much time has elapsed at all. But we live a few hundred miles apart, so it can be hard to find time for a visit.

Our relationship grew very gradually, at first. We lived on a small floor. Maybe eight or ten rooms, with two women each. And so our floor as a unit was very close because it was all women, and we had all chosen to be on an all-women's floor. But I think my link with Janine was really because we were both Christians. That kind of solidified things. Before I went to college I had no background in Christianity, or any religion for that matter. And I became a Christian when I came to college, for various reasons. And Janine had a similar situation. Although she had had some exposure to Christianity as a child, she wasn't really very religious, or just even interested when she was younger. And then her faith and her commitment grew over the years in college. So we shared that.

Amy goes on to talk about what kind of person and friend Janine is. She provides insight into how each of their personalities plays into the dynamics of their friendship:

Janine on the outside is very serious. She's very intellectual and analytical. She spends a lot of time thinking about things, and has a very rich inner world, in terms of her emotions and her thoughts. She is a very artsy person, as well. She loves drama and has a beautiful voice. She's sung in various places, with groups.

I guess she had a similar childhood to mine. Her mom stayed home and was a loving mom who tried to do everything she could for her kids. But Janine experienced some childhood trauma and her experiences of that are things that I can relate to. So I guess in some ways we're very similar, which is probably why we're good friends.

She's a very supportive friend. She'll ask a lot of questions and listen a lot, and not necessarily give a lot of advice or say a lot of what she thinks—mostly trying to get to know how I see the situation and how I feel. She'll definitely share her experiences, but she kind of waits for my lead, as opposed to taking the lead. But I can turn to her for advice if I need it, particularly because she got married a year and a half before I did. She really is, I'd say, my only close married friend. Although I do have other friends that are married, she's really the closest one. And in the beginning of my marriage, I definitely wanted a lot of reassurance. Just basic questions answered that I felt I could ask her because we were similar in a lot of ways and she knew who I was, and had some understanding of who my husband was. And she'd gone through it. Sometimes I talk to her about my sexual relationship with my husband. Mostly general things that are problematic, that relate to other things that she knows about me—aspects of my personality, or my history, or whatever. And she can be very helpful. Sometimes only in the sense of reinforcing my understanding or perspective of the situation, and then other times helpful because she offers a different perspective.

Unfortunately, though, we do have some communication problems. For example, a lot of times, I'll go through a problem, and then after I've resolved it, I'll call her and say, "I've just had this horrible experience," and she'll do the same with me. She'll go through something horrendous and then say, "Yesterday was just awful." And we've talked about how it would be so nice if we could just tell each other in the midst of the problems that something was going on and that we needed a little support. I think that's more a function of both of our personalities and just how we deal with things. We're both kind of stubborn in that way, needing to handle it ourselves. But it would be nice if we could share with each other in the midst of what's going on. And there was actually a period of time when we were roommates, my junior year, when we weren't communicating very well, just because we both don't communicate very well in general. So there were times when we had to talk about that.

But I'd say our relationship has really been a process of sharing more and more. I think we're kind of guarded people in general, and as our lives have changed and as we've grown a little bit, we've been able to share more with each other. So, if anything, I would say that I desire to share more with her, but that that's just a hard thing to do, in general. But I'm learning how to do it.

Nina

As Amy switches over to briefly talk about Nina, we see the appreciation she feels for the different roles Nina plays in Amy's life and for her ability to bring out parts of Amy's personality that are often below the surface:

I met Nina at college also. I guess it was my sophomore year, and she was a year ahead of me. And whereas I'm mostly reserved and kind of quiet, Nina is a very outgoing woman. She loves to laugh and loves to have a lot of fun and just be silly. She's very outgoing, really loves life, and is very vibrant. She really loves new experiences and to meet new people. I think that's what attracted me to her in the beginning.

She is also a Christian and had a really deep faith. And that was another bond for us. And she's got a really serious inner core. She's very pensive and thinks deeply about what's going on in her life and in other people's lives. So we can share in those aspects, as well. But I think Nina really brought out the fun-loving side of me, which I felt very comfortable in sharing with her. And that's a side of me which I didn't feel comfortable sharing with other people. So I think that's part of what solidified my link to her.

But Nina graduated a year before I did, so I guess there were really only two years that I spent with her at college. And since then it's been writing letters mostly. I've seen her occasionally. She was in my wedding, she was in Janine's wedding, and we were all really good friends. Junior year we all lived together in that apartment. Nina, Janine, and I, as well as these two other women. And again it was a very similar kind of situation as with Janine, in that because we were spending so much time with each other, we really shared a lot of our lives. I think early on in the friendships, when I was just forming a relationship with Nina, I was a little jealous of her friendship with Janine, because they had gone to high school together. So they had known each other longer. So I remember feeling jealous about the depth of their relationship and wanting my relationships with them to be very much the same.

Nina's a bit different from Janine in that she's a little less reserved about asking pointed questions or sharing her thoughts about the situation. So she's a little bit more direct. She'll say how she sees a situation pretty frequently. But that's only after having been really supportive and really trying to get the full picture and the story. I really welcome that from her, even as she tells me that she doesn't think what I'm doing is right, because I know that she's really tried to understand the situation before she says, "that sounds nuts." So I appreciate that perspective, because it comes from someone who knows me, who I know cares about me, and who seems to understand the situation.

Janine and Nina

Amy tells the bulk of her story about her friendships not in the individual narratives about each friend, but as she talks about her two friends together. As I discuss in depth in the final section of this chapter, I think her story takes on this structure because although clearly Nina and Janine are different people and different friends to Amy, both fit certain criteria that define best friendship for Amy:

My relationships with Nina and Janine are actually very similar to my relationship with my husband, in that they all know me well and in that we've got some years behind us. So we've seen each other grow over the years. I feel free to be myself, and really share about what's going on in my life. And I'd say with a lot of my other friendships—that may also actually be of as long duration—I don't nec-essarily feel like I can be that open. I don't know if it's that there's a lack of reci-procity in my other relationships or if it's just that I don't feel a click. I don't have that bond with my other friends. And I definitely have other Christian women friends. But it's not the same bond. I guess it's not the same chemistry or mix, or whatever.

I guess in comparing it to a different friend, who fits in that category—Chris-tian woman—with Janine and with Nina, and with my husband, I feel like I can be silly, I can be serious, I can be very upset about something. I can just be whatever emotion I'm feeling when I'm with them. I feel like I can show all sides of myself. Whereas with this other friend or with other friendships, I feel like people maybe know me in a context and I feel sort of confined to act in that context. So, only very serious, or only very silly, or only in a counseling role. That sort of thing. And it's hard to bring in different aspects of myself. Or I feel like I can't bring in those different aspects.

And, actually, although my husband is my best friend, and he is my favorite person in the world, he and I met at the end of my time at college, and because my four years at college were a really formative time for me—that's when I be-came a Christian and a lot of things changed for me—he didn't get to see that. Nina and Janine were there at the time. So I think with both Nina and Janine, I feel like they have a history with me, or I have a history with them. And when I'm with them it reminds me of that. So, looking at my personal development, they were there from the beginning.

With Janine and Nina I also have bonds as women. And I think that just like I can form a bond with someone who is Chinese or a Christian, there is just an in-nately strong bond because of the common ground of being women. My women friendships definitely mean more to me now than friendships with men. There have been times when I've been with groups of women, close friends like Nina or Janine, or also other women friends, where it just feels different than being in a mixed group or being with men. I guess there's an ease to it. I don't feel as guarded, or I don't feel as restrained.

As Amy begins to reflect on another close friendship, we gain a greater understanding about what the defining aspects of best friend-ship are for her:

It's interesting, though, because there's a friendship that I just developed a year and a half ago, and she is, like me, a Christian Chinese woman—Barb. And that friendship got pretty solid, pretty quickly, because of our similar back-grounds and heritage. There were certain things that she would understand with-out my having to explain it, because it reflected being Chinese or having grown up in a certain way. She would know what I was talking about, and that was very nice. That's something that's a little different than with Janine and Nina, who are both white. It's a nice way to relate that I hadn't experienced before.

I was thinking about how I immediately thought of Janine and Nina as my two best friends when I heard about your study, and I've wondered why I didn't think about Barb that way. Because I'd say with Barb, even more so now than with Nina and Janine, the fun side of me that can just sort of joke around and be silly comes out really easily. So it's sort of puzzling to me. But I think that although we have these things in common and we lived near each other—she recently moved—

the immediacy of that friendship wasn't salient enough for me to talk about it the same way. But it's still sort of puzzling to me, because we do have a very close friendship.

And what I do have with Barb, while she was living here anyway, was that we knew sort of the daily things about what was going on in each other's lives. And Janine and I have talked about how when we're together it's so easy to talk about everything—and talk about anything—but when we go for these couple of months when no one has written and no one has called, it's difficult to just pick up the phone and say, "I just had a fight with my husband" or something. We talked about how we wished we were more able to be in contact about the daily things, so that it would be easier to just pick up and call at a random time about a random something or other. If I call now, I think about how I'm going to have to explain all of what's been going on in the last two months before I get her opinion. I was hoping that we would be able to do that over e-mail, but she doesn't really use it. So it is hard.

I think it's that the tie with Janine and Nina as friends is that we have a long friendship and through formative times—our college years and when I became a Christian. And I think that just having been with someone, a friend, through a lot of time or through a lot of different changes, seems more meaningful than a friendship with someone that you are close with but have only known through a certain period of your life. And I've only known Barb for two years, so she's only seen me as a married woman and as a Christian, whereas Janine saw me as a fresh-out-of-high-school, know-nothing non-Christian. And then she saw me become a Christian. And saw me get married. All that kind of stuff. I guess that is what seems like is important for friendship for me. To have an enduring relationship.

Additionally, there are things about me that Janine and Nina know, some of which they were around during, that Barb does not know about. So I feel like Janine and Nina both really know me. I think they can read me really well, and they understand maybe what's behind what I'm saying or doing, without necessarily having to ask about it. So, for example, when I was visiting Janine recently, we were having a conversation, and she knew that I was avoiding something. I think it was partly based on having talked about similar things before, or maybe I had done the same thing before—trying to avoid something—but it wasn't because I was doing anything to suggest that I was avoiding something. But she knew it, and I think that's what I think about when I think about someone knowing me. Whether it's reading my body language or just knowing my personal history and how that affects where I am now, that kind of thing. You know, understanding without having to be told or without having to explain.

And actually that felt great . . . to know that we had a close enough relationship, and that she knew me well enough, to know that I couldn't get away with stuff like that. Whereas some of my friends, here, now, wouldn't have picked up anything and I could have just gone on and wouldn't have been confronted at all. And, maybe that would have been more comfortable, but it was better for her to have confronted me on it. So it felt good. I think that's what close friendships are about—when someone feels understood by the other person, and the understanding goes beyond words. Things don't need to be said. I think that's a lot of the reason for why I feel comfortable with them. Because I know that they understand who I am and understand things about me, so I don't feel awkward because I'm not known.

It's interesting because I don't have that as much with Barb as with Janine and Nina. I think that sharing those things—specifically, experiences of having been violated, in a sexual way—explains a lot. And so, for example, one of the things that was really difficult for me about where I live is that I'd be trying to go buy milk and I'd be getting a lot of comments from men, really lewd things, and people approaching me and all that kind of stuff. And that was a really hard thing to deal with on a day-to-day basis. I know that if I were to say that to Janine, she would understand what I meant and why it was so difficult for me to deal with someone saying, "Hey baby." Whereas I've said that to Barb before, and Barb doesn't know about my history, so she doesn't quite understand why it's such a difficult thing for me to deal with. I mean she understands just being a woman that it's difficult to deal with stuff like that, but I think she doesn't really fully understand why it's so devastating to me sometimes. She was actually with me once and something happened, and I lost it, and she didn't really know how to respond. But I know that if Janine had been there, she would have known exactly what was going on. I think at some point I'll probably tell Barb, but I think I haven't yet because I know that she hasn't had that experience, so it's just not that easy to say.

Amy's feeling of connection with Nina and Janine as women who have experienced some kind of sexual violation and daily experience objectification that her husband cannot understand is on a level with her connection with them as born-again Christians:

With both Nina and Janine, at various points in our lives, we've talked about sexuality and different sexual things—I think because we've shared similar traumatic experiences. That's something that Janine and I actually talk about pretty frequently, I'd say. We talk about hang-ups or whatever, because of our past experiences. And I can remember conversations with Nina about being a woman and how men respond to women in a sexual way. I can remember this one conversation in which she had been leered at by some passerby and was devastated. I could relate to her feelings in terms of being treated as an object—as just body parts and that sort of thing. We talked a lot about that. Just having had those experiences so many times, it was something that we could share with each other.

I've talked to my husband about all these things, but because Janine and Nina have experienced it, they can, I think, relate in a deeper way than my husband can. He can understand it cognitively, and I'm sure emotionally he can understand it a little too, but because he hasn't had that experience, I know he doesn't understand as deeply as Janine and Nina do. His initial reaction is to get pretty angry. And he pretty much just stays angry. He's very empathic with me, in the sense that he knows that I'm upset and so he's sad for me. But I think that he doesn't experience the feeling of being objectified. He doesn't feel that same sense of being victimized. So whereas I know I could give an example to Janine and she would just know what I was talking about, I think my husband doesn't feel that sense as much. I don't know if he feels it at all, actually.

Amy's narrative ends as it begins—with an emphasis on the role her faith plays in her life and her relationships—and on the faith she has in the strength of those relationships:

But what I have with all three of them—Janine, Nina, and Barb—as well as with my husband, that I don't have with some of my other friends, is that we are all Christians. So that when I'm having a conversation with Janine, or Nina, or Barb, and I'm talking about something—maybe something simple like there's a difficult work situation, or something more complicated like I'm confused about my life—it's so much more reassuring to pray about it than to just leave it as, "Uh, well sorry, can't help you, I don't know what to do about it either."

So many other things in our lives are out of our control. As much as we would try to control them, they're really just out of our control. And when I pray, essentially what I'm doing is coming before God and saying, "My life is a mess, this is bad and this is bad, and I need help. And, so I'm just going to leave this here with you, and I'll just wait to see what you're going to do with it." So when I'm praying with one of my friends, it's the same sort of idea. We've shared concerns and we've shared problems, and as friends we're going before God and kind of laying them down before God and saying, "Here's our mess. Can you do something about it? Because we can't. And it's out of our control and we don't really know what to do." So I think that's really why it's important for me to pray with my friends. And by praying together, it also feels like someone else is coming alongside to help you through it, by praying for you.

Although I have some good friends that are not Christian, I don't think I can be as intimate with someone who is not a Christian. I think that after experiencing friendships like I have with Janine and Nina, where we can share about what's going on and then we can pray for each other, I would find it hard to have the same level of intimacy with someone who I couldn't do that with. For example, I might be going through something, and Janine or Nina could say to me something biblical, like, "That reminds me of this verse" and offer me comfort in that way. I wouldn't necessarily receive that from someone who wasn't Christian. And because I derive my comfort and my security and all that from my Christian faith and my relationship with God, and it's such an integral part of my life and who I am, I feel that it would be hard to have intimacy without that, with another woman.

And when I think of these two friendships, I think of them as really enduring. I think that with both of them, there's a deep core that endures. So as we change, we can adapt to the changes in each other and still be close friends, because there's a base, strong relationship. Although I'm sure that we could grow apart, it doesn't worry me that much, maybe because there have been periods when we have been apart. For example, Nina was overseas for almost a year. So obviously I didn't see her then and didn't call her then. I got a couple of letters, but it was sporadic. But after that year, when she came back and I saw her, it was as if he had never left. So I feel like if time elapses or situations change, because of that basic core, we could go back to establishing a strong friendship again even if we'd grown apart. I guess my only concerns are when I have realized that I haven't called or written in awhile. I feel like I need to do that to maintain the friendship. I want to make sure that I am holding up my end in terms of keeping contact. These friendships are just very special, and I don't know how many people really get to experience deep friendships in this way. I feel very blessed that I have these two women friends and my husband.

FURTHER REFLECTIONS:
WHAT MAKES A BEST FRIEND?

When I consider Amy's two interviews together, I see that from beginning to end she painted a picture that enabled me to understand why these two friendships are, for her, best friendships. Janine and Nina both have four attributes that seem to define for Amy why they are her best friends: (1) they are women, (2) they are Christian, (3) they have experienced some kind of sexual violation, and (4) they have known Amy since right before or right after she became a Christian, as her faith was really developing. It is impossible to know, of course, whether these attributes came to define best friendship for Amy because her two best friends had them or if the process was reversed—that is, if these defining attributes caused Amy to choose Janine and Nina as best friends. Both processes were likely involved.

Amy makes it clear throughout our interviews that she has come to value female friendship more than male friendship. That her friends are both women, as is she, provides an "innately strong bond." In fact, at one point she says that she has no desire to form close friendships with men, although she does not dismiss the possibility that she could have an intimate friendship with a man other than her husband:

P: Would you be able to have an intimate friendship with a man?

A: I think I would be able to, but I don't know if I would want to.

P: Why not?

A: I think because I see my husband as my primary male friendship and don't feel necessarily a need to go beyond that. There's not something that I feel like a friendship with a male could meet that a friendship with Nina or Janine or somebody else couldn't meet. So why bring that into the occasion, you know? It just adds unwanted tension, unwanted stress or something.

Being friends with women seems to allow Amy to relax and not worry about the tensions—presumably sexual—that accompany friendship with men. She reiterates this sentiment when she says that being in a mixed gender group feels different from being in an all-female group—she doesn't have to feel as guarded when she is with just women. And, it was the single-sexed freshman year floor that provided an environment where her friendships with other women could more readily be cultivated.

The theme of Amy's religious faith runs throughout the story of her friendships. On a very basic level, it gave her contact with Janine and Nina because they were all involved in Christian organizations on campus. Then, at least with Janine, as their faith grew, so did a strong area of commonality between them. They experienced change together, and it became a shared bond among all of them. Amy says that she cannot imagine attaining the same level of closeness with someone who is not Christian. It strikes me that her times of joint prayer with her friends are moments of great intimacy. In the following passage, Amy describes her weekly prayer meetings with Barb:

> We'd tell each other what was going on in our lives and then I would pray for Barb's concerns and she would pray for mine. And in that process, sometimes we'd pray for ourselves. I guess a part of it is to feel that someone else is coming alongside to help you through it, by praying for you. And you're not the only one trying to deal with things.

They are sharing with each other what is going on in their lives, and they are coming together toward a shared goal of getting help from God.

The third area of commonality between Amy and her friends is that they have all experienced some form of sexual violation. Amy explains that their shared history strengthens the bond of understanding among the three of them. Janine and Nina know in a way others cannot what it is like for Amy when someone makes a lewd remark to her. In addition, Amy says she feels that Janine can offer advice or comfort regarding aspects of Amy's sexual relationship with her husband because Janine knows where Amy's "hang-ups" originate. Without that understanding, as we can see in the case of Amy's friendship with Barb, a key ingredient is missing. Not only does Amy feel incompletely understood by Barb—and possibly misunderstood—but she, herself, is not allowing Barb to see the entire picture. She feels she is not being entirely herself with Barb, and Amy thus does not feel that she can call Barb a best friend.

Finally, what Janine and Nina can offer in their friendships that no one else can is that they have known Amy through different periods of time in her life and, in particular, dating from the time when she was developing her faith. Janine, in fact, knew her when she was a "know-nothing . . . non-Christian." Amy places a great deal of importance on being known, and Janine and Nina know her in ways no one else does: they know her now, they knew her before she was who she is now (i.e., before she became a Christian), and they witnessed the transformation. Amy's husband and Barb met Amy only after she had become a Christian. (See Chapter 11 for an in-depth discussion of knowing.)

Chapter 8

"I Can Count on My Best Friend . . . Not That I Would": The Conundrum of Independence versus Dependence

Once upon a time, a feminist psychologist at Harvard University named Carol Gilligan was at the forefront of a revolution—a revolution that opened the door for understanding how women conceptualize the world around them. In 1982, when Gilligan published her book *In a Different Voice,* a chorus of sighs could be heard around the nation as the first group of female readers turned the last page on a book they were likely to read several more times.[1] Why? Because Gilligan showed us that the renowned theorists Jean Piaget and Lawrence Kohlberg, whose theories of child development and moral thinking were considered near gospel, had largely misrepresented 51 percent of the population. Based on Piagetian research, which in turn was based almost entirely on boys, Kohlberg developed a scale of moral development. Consequently, when this scale is used, women rarely are seen to reach the top levels of moral thinking. Not only have Kohlberg's theories no doubt left many a female psychology student feeling rather inadequate, they have greatly influenced the fields of child and personal development.

Then came Gilligan, who said, Wait. What if we were to look at all of this with a different lens? What if we were to view the way women think as just different—not better or worse? (Although those reading Gilligan's work will not doubt that she was somewhat biased toward one way of thinking.) Based on her own research, Gilligan saw that while men tend to see things as primarily black and white, women see the grays in between. While men's thinking is often linear, women's is circular. And while men often find it intolerable to hold apparently contradictory beliefs, for women such is a normal state of being.

All of which brings us to the subject matter at hand: The women I talked to repeatedly said that their friends "would always be there for them." Best friends are friends we absolutely know we can count on. What could be more straightforward than that? But let us remember who we're dealing with here—not those linear thinkers. It turns out, that many of those women who are sure that their friends will appear at their doorstep at a moment's notice, are extraordinarily reluctant to test that certainty. In other words, they love that their friends are there for them, but they really, really do not want to have to ask them to be there. (Do I detect a slight movement of the earth as a multitude of women are nodding their heads in self-recognition?) Alice, Linda, and Nancy provide three examples of how these seemingly contradictory impulses can manifest themselves.

ALICE

I'm very conscious of not wanting to be too dependent.

Although Alice greatly values her friendship with Julia, there are certain aspects that she finds problematic and would like to change. For the most part, these are related to difficulties in communication. Alice and Julia have been friends since the fifth grade, and Alice thinks that some of the problems they have may be rooted in their early friendship. For example, Alice worried about asking too much of Julia because of the difficulties Julia faced at home:

> I guess another facet of our relationship, or at least of me in our relationship, is that I worry about being too demanding as a friend. I think this really goes back to our childhood, because I was very aware of Julia having demands on her—like at home, and then in her marriage—that kind of occupied a lot of energy and stuff. And I just worried about being too demanding. I think I still do.

Alice explains that she did not feel free to ask Julia for help. She also hesitated to talk to Julia about her concerns regarding the friendship because she did not want to add to Julia's overall burden. Later, after Julia seemed unhappily married to her high school teacher, Alice was again wary of placing additional demands on her friend.

As Alice points out, these issues have carried over into their current relationship. For example, Alice felt hurt when Julia did not stop by to see her when she was in town recently, but saying anything to Julia seemed too difficult. Alice was also concerned that she was being too sensitive:

> Since we get to see each other so rarely and—I know it's because they're busy . . . and I know I tend to be a little sensitive to things like that too.

But since Alice remained bothered by the incident, she decided to write to Julia to express her feelings. She had a difficult time telling Julia how she felt because she could not help but worry, once again, that Julia had too many demands on her—this time stemming from her work and her marriage.

Alice is concerned that Julia tends to emotionally distance herself when she is going through difficult times. According to Alice:

> What happens is that when her self-esteem issues start coming up, she won't call or be in touch. And she and her husband have a lot of financial difficulties, and when that sort of stuff starts coming up as well, she'll be out of touch. That's kind of what's happening now.

When I ask Alice why she thinks Julia reacts this way, she responds that Julia is concerned about becoming a burden to Alice. Apparently, this is a pattern that began during Julia's first marriage. Julia pulled away from Alice at that time under the influence of her domineering husband, while Alice struggled, to some extent, to maintain contact. When Alice thinks back on that period, she wishes that she had found a way to assert herself and be there for Julia. Alice feels guilty that she failed her friend in her time of need.

Clearly, Alice and Julia find it extraordinarily difficult to show that they need each other. As Alice describes it, much of this has to do with the difficulties Julia has had throughout her life. Alice does not want to put additional pressure on Julia because Julia has enough to deal with. Julia, in turn, does not want to further burden Alice because she views herself as having continually been in a state of need.

What further complicates the dynamic, however, is that each wants to be there for the other. Of Julia, Alice says:

So this has been going on for a long, long time, for years. And she's very quick to want to be of help to me, but it almost seems like she's not comfortable asking for help, or just talking about what's on her mind.

This is obviously frustrating to Alice. When I ask how she responds when Julia says that she does not want to be a burden, she replies:

"You're not. You're my oldest and dearest friend in the world, and I want to know what's going on with you and I want to hear everything." I feel really sad about it, but I also understand it, because I think I'm that way too a little bit. I'm very conscious of not wanting to be too . . . dependent . . . maybe? Or I have this thing about not wanting to add to people's problems.

Overall, however, Alice feels that of the two of them, she is the one to reach out more often. Although she is conscious of not wanting to be too demanding, she is able to overcome those concerns when it is important enough to her—when she really needs her best friend or when she feels she has to let Julia know that she is hurt. She wishes, however, that she could convince Julia to do the same. Alice is clearly very conscious of the contradictory desires that exist within her friendship with Julia, and she strives, to some degree, to alleviate her resulting feelings of discomfort.

LINDA

A best friend really would do anything, providing it wasn't too wild. But if you called them up and said, "I need a favor," they would do it. Even if it meant taking a day off of work. If you said, "I just need you. You have to come over today." I think both of them would do that. As I would do for them. I think I would assume that they would be there for me, whatever that means.

For Linda, a best friend is someone who will be there for her should she ever ask. But Linda explains that, in truth, she would never put her friends in such a position:

> They don't have to be there for me, because I'm not demanding. I would never—I've never asked them to do that. I'm not the type to say, "Oh, I'm falling apart, you have to come over."

Linda says she does not like to unload her problems on others. She sees herself as very different from women who do lean on their friends:

> I've heard of women who go over and stay all night with a friend for three days for some reason. I would never ask someone to do something like that for me. I guess in a way I'm very independent.

In turn, Linda likes friends who are not too needy. At one point, she had a friend who always needed to be with people. Her best friends, Emily and Carol, are not like that: "Maybe we're all the same type, not being real needy people. Or not being people that need someone around all the time."

Perhaps because Linda talked so much about this topic, I wondered if she worried that she would ever be perceived as needy. She seemed to be expending a great deal of effort—in her relationship with Emily, in particular—ensuring that her self-sufficiency could not be missed. When I asked her if that was the case, she said that she does worry about that "a little bit, I think . . . I think a little bit." I always wondered if in her endeavor to be viewed as independent—such as when she resists calling Emily even when she would like to—a price might be being paid. Wouldn't she feel better if she just gave in to her desire to pick up the phone? However, Linda told me that there is nothing about her friendship with Emily that she would want to change. And she certainly makes it clear that she is comfortable keeping emotional distance in her relationships. Thus, although I felt saddened by what I viewed as her self-imposed emotional isolation—perhaps recognizing a bit too well that deeply ingrained desire to avoid any perception of neediness—she seemed to be more comfortable operating that way.

Nevertheless, Linda acknowledges that she may be fearful of rejection:

> So if I don't show you too much, that I need you too much, then you can't reject me. And I feel that more with Em. Actually I

feel I would want to be with her more than I would want to be with Carol, so I think rejection by Em would hurt more than rejection by Carol.

One of the questions I had after reviewing our first interview was: How does she know that her friends will be there for her if she never asks them to be? When I bring this up during our second interview, she explains that both Carol and Emily have "said it" to her. But I think there is more to it than that. There is a mutual understanding in both of these friendships—a firm belief that each person will be there for the other. Moreover, this understanding is due, in part, to the fact that they *rarely* call upon one another:

> We don't do hundreds of favors. You know, if she calls and says, "Look, I'm really stuck. Can you pick me up at the airport?" I would say yes. I would do everything I could, because I knew that I would be the last one she would ask, in a way. Because she knew I wouldn't say no.

Thus, Linda believes that there are two major tacit understandings in both friendships. First, neither party places many, if any, demands on the other, and second, if a request is made, it is urgently needed.

Linda notes that when she and Emily lived close to each other, Emily would ask for favors; however, Carol, who is now her neighbor, never does. Linda believes that Carol, though very independent, may be taking her cue from Linda in this regard. They now have developed a dynamic in which it is very difficult to ask even for small favors, such as getting a lift to the car mechanic. Linda says that sometimes she sees Carol taking cabs and wishes Carol would just ask her for a ride. Linda then admits that she would be more inclined to ask Carol for a favor if Carol approached her first. Linda would like to break down this barrier, but she is not quite sure how to go about it: "I guess maybe I should say something to her, like, 'you know, I would give you a ride if you called me up,' but *she* never does" [emphasis added]. It was striking to me that Linda switched from "I" to "she" in this statement, highlighting her antipathy toward being the one to ask for help.

Yet, while she and her friends are reluctant to reach out to one another for help, Linda feels sure that both Emily and Carol would be there for her if she needed them. She knows that they have the same certainty about her: "I guess it's just unspoken that we would do anything for each other. We just know that if we needed something, we could call and they would be there." Thus, Linda's best friendships very much exist between those clearly defined blacks and whites; however, but for some pangs here and there, Linda is not altogether uncomfortable residing there.

NANCY

> I kind of depend on myself. It's just a style. I think that's just how I've always been.

In contrast to Linda and Alice, Nancy seems pretty comfortable with what she perceives as her independent personality and how that works for her in her relationships. While Linda, too, says that she is independent, she intimates that she sometimes wishes it were easier for her to reach out to her friends. Nancy seems far more matter-of-fact about the way she is. When I ask her who she turns to when she needs somebody, she responds:

> That's a good question. You know, that's a trait about me that irks both Claudia and Lisa. Both of them have brought it up with me, and other people have brought it up, as well. I'm more of a person who relies on myself.

Unlike Linda, Nancy says that she is very much able to ask for help for what she calls "instrumental things," such as getting a ride somewhere. But when she is having a personal problem, she chooses not to talk about it. She says this is "just her style."

Nancy explains that good friends of hers over the years have pointed this trait out to her with frustration. She remembers that her best friend in high school would get mad at her for just this reason:

P: Why do you think people get mad at you for that?

N: A piece of it is, people have said they would like to help me, and have the opportunity to help me like I've helped them. Or, what's the matter? Don't I think that they are my very good friend? Why wouldn't I think I could depend on them? I guess they get insulted.

Obviously, Nancy has listened to her friends, and she seems to understand their points of view; yet she has not changed what she calls her style. She can, however, see ways in which that style might not always serve her well. As an example of this, she explains that in the incident with Lisa and Valerie, if she had explained to Lisa how she felt, Lisa might have handled the situation better:

N: On some level I didn't tell Lisa outright what I needed from her. I didn't quite know how to do it, or I just didn't do it. And I could see her getting caught up in her own stuff. She was caught in what was good for her career versus our friendship. I didn't give her the benefit of the doubt and let her work it out. I just said, "Fine, you deal with your career," and didn't tell her anything. But Lisa tried. A piece of it was I didn't help her.

P: So it sounds like in hindsight you figured that out. That you had a part in how Lisa acted.

N: Well, yeah, at that time I could've told you I had a part in it. I'm reflective enough to know my style. Not that I don't get frustrated with other people for not just figuring it out, and why didn't they just do it, but it certainly is something that's been pointed out to me. Claudia pointed it out to me when I was nineteen. It's been a concern of hers for years.

Thus, Nancy sees her own complicity.

As with Linda, after Nancy tells me that she can always rely on her friends, she immediately explains that she would never do so. She is talking here first about Claudia:

> I could go visit her any time I needed to. And that would be fine. Though it's not something that I would do. And Lisa's also the same way. I could call Lisa whenever I wanted to. If I needed help, I could count on both of them. *Not that I would, but I could* [emphasis added].

This statement is striking. While Nancy is certain she can depend on her friends, she is equally certain that she would never do so. During the second interview, I remember how she had stressed earlier that she did not turn to her friends. I ask her how she can thus be certain that her friends would come through:

> Because I just . . . know. Things that they've offered, things that they've done for me in the past. I don't know, I just know. I guess there are people about whom you just don't know that, but then they wouldn't be your very good friend. Because you wouldn't know them well enough to know that.

Although Nancy cannot imagine a situation—not even a crisis situation—in which she would need her friends' help, the absolute certainty that they would be there if she ever did is, without doubt, an integral part of these relationships. Of the three women discussed here (Alice, Linda, and Nancy), Nancy is clearly the most at ease with her choice of residence—once again, that gray area of inconsistency.

REFLECTIONS

Carol Gilligan may be right that women do not feel the need to reconcile apparently contradictory views and desires, but that does not mean that we do not have some inner conflict as a result. Balancing our need for connection and emotional intimacy with a desire to be seen as independent and self-reliant can be very difficult.

As I was examining the women's words, I found three threads that ran throughout the discussions on this topic. First, the women expressed discomfort with feelings of dependence (as we saw with Alice and Linda) and affirmed their own independence (as with Linda and Nancy). Second, the women very much wanted their friends to lean on them (as we saw with Nancy's friends and Alice). And, finally, all of the women had an unwavering belief that their friends would be there when called upon, even if they never put them to the test. The question inevitably emerges, why is there so much pushing and pulling going on here?

Virtually everybody born and raised in our culture learns that dependency is not a state we should strive for as we get older. To say that someone is dependent is to imply that she is childlike or lacking in a significant trait marking adulthood. Psychoanalysis views dependency as having its origin in the oral stage—the first stage of development. An individual with an oral personality is generally described as dependent and infantile. What's more, the psychiatric literature does not differentiate between pathological and normal dependency. According to Stiver:

Essentially, the prevailing belief seems to be that dependency needs belong in childhood, and if these needs, whatever they are, are not satisfied in childhood, they continue to exert influences in a negative fashion, either in the form of counter-dependent personalities . . . or more directly in the form of clinging, demanding, helpless personalities.[2]

Stiver believes that dependency "has acquired such pejorative connotations precisely because it has been considered for so long to be a feminine characteristic."[3]

Based on our culture's attitude toward this trait, it is not surprising to find that many women cannot bear to be viewed as needy. In a culture that emphasizes "standing on one's own two feet," dependency is certainly not considered an attractive attribute in adulthood. For the women in this study, however, the idea could be expected to cause particular dissonance. All the participants have taken substantive steps toward self-sufficiency. Five of the seven women are pursuing doctorates. Of the remaining two, one already has a doctorate and one has a master's degree. Those who are not yet financially independent are moving in that direction. Thus, according to most societal definitions, these women are probably highly motivated to be independent, at least in a specific, public area of their lives. In fact, it may be that many of these women place an even higher value on independence than we might expect of women in general. It is therefore not surprising to find that many of the women had difficulty reconciling their desire to feel independent with their longing for a close, intimate relationship.

This brings us to the second thread I uncovered. While many of the women feel uncomfortable leaning on their friends, they absolutely want their friends to turn to them. Feminist theorists write about an *ethic of care* that exists among women. For many women, being in a valued relationship involves choosing to care for another. And that caring evokes a deep empathy. More specifically, to care deeply, women strive to feel what the other feels—to understand an experience as another does. Nel Noddings, a philosopher, writes that caring of this nature involves taking on the other person's reality and behaving accordingly.[4] In other words, the line between acting on one's own behalf and acting on the other's becomes blurred. Interestingly, at the same time that an ethic of care has traditionally been devalued in our culture, as well as in psychological theory, women are expected to—and do—define and judge themselves according to their ability to care.

A desire to care certainly comes through in many of these stories. It bothers Alice, for instance, that Julia worries about being a burden. The fact that Julia has a tendency to "be out of touch" at the times when she is having the greatest difficulties is very upsetting to Alice. She wants to help Julia and wishes Julia felt comfortable coming to her. In contrast, it is not Nancy, but Nancy's friends who express frustration at not being allowed to care for their friend. Nancy says that her friends get angry because although she is very willing to help them, she does not allow them to help her. Also, Liz, who was not discussed earlier, says that something is missing in her relationship with Sandy because she feels that Sandy does not really need her.

> I guess because she's so independent, sometimes I have difficulty with that relationship in that it lacks the kind of recognition you get through knowing that someone needs you. She's so much on her own in a lot of ways. Sometimes I find that difficult. But it's not that I feel like she doesn't tell me things. I actually feel like she does tell me a lot of very personal things. But there's never that real emotional quality.

All of these women feel that to some extent the relationships are not altogether healthy and whole if they are not allowed the opportunity to care for their friends. In addition, it is interesting that in their attempt to avoid dependence, Nancy and Linda, in particular, do not acknowledge their own need to be cared for.

None of the participants doubted that their best friend would be available in their time of need. In fact, this conviction seems to be a defining factor of best friendship between women. Yet the following question naturally arises: Why do women who feel certain that they would *never* call on their friends, feel so strongly that they must know that they *can* do so? Here we have the third thread.

As we have seen, women highly value their ability to care for others within a relationship. It does not seem surprising, therefore, that the participants would feel it essential that their best friends possess this ethic of care. Women need to know that their friends are emotionally dependable and available—just as they, themselves, are. This certainty may also serve as something of a safety net. For instance, women are usually the emotional caretakers in heterosexual relationships. Furthermore, many of the participants feel that their husbands or lovers do not understand them in the way that their best friends do. Since caring necessarily involves a deep understanding of the other, many women may not trust that their male partners will provide the sort of help and support they feel they need. Thus, their confidence in their friends provides a sense of security and a peace of mind.

Gilligan writes:

> [W]hile women have . . . taken care of men, men have, in their theories of psychological development, as in their economic arrangements, tended to assume or devalue that care. When the focus on individuation and individual achievement extends into adulthood and maturity is equated with personal autonomy, concern with relationships appears as a weakness of women rather than as a human strength. . . .[5]

In other words, although women are expected to be the caretakers of relationships, their ability to do so is not valued. The truth is, an adult's success in life is not measured by his or her success in relationships—the very concept seems almost laughable. Furthermore, if women actually do focus on their own needs and look to others for support, they are likely to feel even more inadequate, because they will be viewed as weak and deficient, lacking a trait that defines maturity and adulthood.

Placed in the context of our culture's attitudes, the difficulties women have negotiating these issues of independence are not surprising. Women receive mixed messages throughout their lives about which behaviors and feelings are valued. While they are taught to be caring, supportive, and empathetic, they are also told that if they seek help from others they will appear needy and dependent—in other words, childlike. When two women come together to form a close, intimate relationship, it seems almost inevitable that confusion, conflict, and ambivalence surrounding these issues will develop.

Chapter 9

Deb

Deb is a fifty-four-year-old white middle-class woman with a doctorate. She is married for the second time and has two adult children. Both of our interviews took place in her office. I was in a chair next to her desk, and she sat in her desk chair facing me. Before the start of both interviews, she pushed her chair a few feet away from the desk, so we ended up sitting about six feet apart.

Soon after I entered Deb's office for the first interview and we exchanged pleasantries, I asked her if she had read the informed consent form that I had sent her. She said that she had and that she had some questions about it. She asked me why I was not interviewing her and her best friend together and whether I would talk to her friend at all. When I told her I would not, she said that that did not make sense to her, because without talking to Gina, I would not get a complete picture of the friendship. She pointed out that the friendship was "dialogic." I explained my many reasons for not interviewing both partners, and I explained that although what she was suggesting would certainly yield an interesting picture of the friendship, it was a different one than I was currently looking at. Deb brought the subject up on several occasions over the course of the study.

I had mechanical difficulties in the taping of my first two interviews with Deb and lost about half of each interview. However, I reconstructed the interviews to the best of my abilities as soon as I realized what had happened. (Qualitative researchers often do not tape record their participants, and I, fortunately, had been trained to gather data without doing so.) I conducted a third interview with Deb—this time over the phone—to fill in some gaps.

THE STORY

Deb's best friendship with Gina spans a period of almost three de-cades, beginning in young adulthood for both of them. We thus get a peek at a friendship growing and changing as the friends, themselves, grow and change:

I moved into a new home about twenty-seven years ago, and Gina lived across the street. We both had little boys. Dan, my son, was a newborn and Sam, Gina's son, was two. When the boys were young, we would get together all the time at one of our houses and they would play. We would do all kinds of things to-gether. We would sit and talk. And when Gina and I were going through difficult times, we would take out coloring books and crayons and just color together for hours. We would laugh about it, but we found it very therapeutic just to do that to-gether.

Humor is an important part of the friendship. We really connect on that level. My father had a very similar kind of humor to Gina. They're very dry. It's kind of seeing things that are humorous in everyday events. I don't have that in any of my other friendships—that level of connection. Maybe with my sons—because they have a sense of humor like my father did. Gina's also like my father in that she defuses a lot of things with her humor. Like if I'm being serious or talking about getting old or something, she'll defuse the moment with a joke. My father did that, but he did it too much. He couldn't talk on a serious level at all, while Gina can do both.

Over the twenty-seven years, we've been through a lot together. A lot of life crises and life events. We've each been divorced and remarried. She was there for the birth of my second child. Our children have grown up together. She was there when my father died. She was there when I got my dissertation done and when I did a presentation for an advance in my career. I invited her to come to that. We've just seen each other through a lot of things.

More recently, Gina's had to deal with her son being sick. He had cancer and had to have chemo. He was home recently and was pretty depressed about hav-ing to now have radiation. And it's been hard for her. So I've just tried to listen and basically respond when asked, not try to solve it, because there's really not any solving to be done. It's a time of being able to be present with each other. That's what I think she needs. This is one of those times when I wish she were here, be-cause then she could say if that's not what she needs. She could tell me what she really needs.

One of the things we've done together every year over the years is to go away. We go to the beach for a weekend every year. We began when my youngest son was two. It's something we just need to do. We need to go away together and just relax. It feels different now than it used to, because we're different. But it's still very important. When the kids were young, we needed time away from them and from the family. Sometimes now when we make plans, we give our husbands an option to come. Sometimes they do, but usually they don't. When we go away, it's a relief to be able to go for walks and not be worried about by Bob, my husband. I like to take walks at night, and he worries about me. Sometimes he wants to go with me, or he follows me because he worries that someone will hurt me. So it's nice when we're away to just be able to take a walk without thinking about whether he's worried about me. And it's a time just to be. It's rejuvenating to be able to let down and be myself for a few days, which I can do when I'm with Gina.

When we go, Gina and I don't spend all our time together. In fact, we spend much of the day apart, doing different things and going different places. But at the end of the day, we always get together and cook dinner. And then we just sit and eat dinner and talk. At first, we really had to check in with each other to make sure it was OK to spend time apart. We both very much need space and are cognizant of the other's needing space, but it was a little difficult at first to do that. We kept checking in and asking the other one if it was really OK. But now we don't need to do that. It's just very comfortable, and we each go off and do our own thing. I think over time and with age we've just grown more trusting and more comfortable. And I think the defining factor of our friendship is the trust, earned over time. We've been friends for so many years that it's like we've grown up together.

At earlier points in the friendship, we had some misunderstandings when we would have plans to do something together and then would call each other to change them because it seemed really important to do something with our husbands. There would be some hurt feelings. But we talked that through at some point after we each remarried. And after we talked about it directly, it became less of a chafing kind of thing. It was a difficult conversation at the time, but it cleared things up. And it helped develop trust. We knew we could be honest and share how we were feeling. That trust developed gradually over the years of the friendship because it was earned.

It is interesting to reflect on a friendship and look for the circumstances that enabled its development. Deb is very clear that if she and Gina had met in another context, it is unlikely they would have the relationship they have today:

I don't think the relationship would have become what it did if we hadn't been neighbors. The proximity was very important. If we had lived further away, I just don't think we would have made the effort. We both are homebodies. We don't really like to travel. So I don't think it would have happened. The trust wouldn't have had an opportunity to develop. Also, Gina and I used to meet halfway in the street all the time. If one of us was upset, we'd call the other one and just meet halfway and hug and cry. We used to do that all the time, particularly when we were going through rough times. And then maybe we'd say we'd meet later for a drink or whatever. We didn't care who was around or what people might think. In fact, one of our neighbors, whose husband was actually gay, asked us if we were more than just friends. And another woman in the neighborhood asked us also. And we talked about it with these two people. It was interesting to think of ourselves in that way. We talked about it a little, but that just wasn't a part of the relationship. And we just basically decided we didn't care what other people might think. We finally just decided that people could think whatever they thought. And we would hug a lot, walk arm in arm, and hold hands at parties. I mean it's always been comfortable, but it evolved to be more publicly comfortable.

Inevitably, Deb and Gina have had to negotiate their relationship and the time they want to be together with the needs and desires of others in their lives:

We've each faced some protestation about the friendship from our husbands at one time or another. When women have a good friendship it often has to be fought for. My first husband had some jealousy, but he came to understand. And then my second husband also had a difficult time with it, but he now sees how good it is for me, even if he doesn't completely understand. He really only has one friend, a "locker room"-type friend, so he doesn't have friends the way I do. It was hard for him to understand, at first, why I needed to have a friend like Gina in my life, when I had him. We had to negotiate within the relationship that I needed some time away from him, for my friendship—and for my kids. And what does it mean in his life if I have all these other things and he does not? But now he really does embrace it. I think that both Bob and Jimmy, Gina's husband, though they might think they're not supposed to be relieved and glad that we have this friendship, they are. They seem to be glad that we like doing what we do together, because they don't want to do it with us. But it can still be a struggle sometimes because they feel competitive about the friendship. And they don't understand why we have to see each other every week.

She's also a friend to my children. My children rely on her being in my life. They're glad. I'm not sure they always were. I think that sometimes when they were little kids they might have felt like they wanted me to be with them and I chose to be with her. But now they seem to know what she means to me. Dan, my oldest son, gives me a trip to see him every year, with Gina. So we go and visit him and we all have brunch together. I feel like they always had access to Gina. And I think that they might go to her and ask her if they were too vulnerable to ask me about something. Whereas I don't have as close a relationship with Gina's son, Sam. I don't usually visit with her when Sam is visiting. And I'm trying to imagine how Sam feels about the friendship. Maybe he would come to me if he needed something. I don't know. I know that in birthday cards and remembrances of important events, Sam has said what it means to him that his mother and I are friends. So maybe he does feel close to me.

As Deb talks at length about what she gets from the relationship, we see just how integral Gina is to Deb's life:

Gina and I talk a lot about our husbands and our marriages and how we're feeling. We talk things through with each other. When we were younger, the responses—well, I'll just talk about myself—my response was often an advocacy of her position, because I'd usually agree with what she was saying. If I didn't agree, I would say, "Well, I don't think he really meant that" or "I had that happen with my husband, and when I'd press him on it, he didn't really mean it that way." But now I find that we can be both advocates and imagine the other person's side. For example, Gina's been very helpful in doing that when I'm very angry at my husband, and she'll say, "Gee, he must be really depressed about that" or "He's thinking about retiring." But sometimes that isn't what I want. I don't want her to think about his side. And if that's the way I feel, I'll tell her, "I don't really want to hear that right now" or "It's still too new for me to hear you be on his side. I just need you to be on my side" or whatever. But most times I do really like that she's able to help me see his side. Because I know she's my advocate. I mean I just know that. In fact, that is her advocating.

My friendship with Gina has opened the door to other relationships in my life. For instance, it's helped me build a relationship with my sister. I used to worry that I was substituting my relationship with Gina for what I should have with my sister. And I felt bad that I wasn't as close to my sister as I was to Gina. But through the friendship, and in therapy, I was able to find a way to develop that relationship. And recently, I felt encouraged by trips with Gina to try taking a trip with my sister, which was wonderful. We had a wonderful time. I was also able to talk to my mother about some things because of a comment she made about my relationship with Gina. While I was going through my divorce, she asked me if I was doing this because Gina was also getting divorced. I couldn't believe she would think that, and I just thought it said a lot about what my mother thought about me. But it gave me an opening to talk to my mother about her feelings about the divorce, which was very hard on her.

Gina's just really important for me to have in my life. She's a very constant friend. She's a very reliable person. Honest, funny. She's just a delightful person. I'm really glad she's in my life. Recently, though, she moved away. And that was very difficult. Her husband and she bought a house about six minutes away. That continues in some ways to be hard. It was very hard for us to move away. I find myself doing fewer things in the front of my house. I have a screened-in back porch now, which was built around the time when they were thinking about moving. It's weird, but I'm just thinking about that now as I'm talking. I used to sit out front more. Now, I'll take the garbage out and see the light on in various parts of the house across the street and there'll be memories. . . . I'll remember things.

She was recently telling me that for a long time it was hard for her at her house to not have access right across the street and watch what was happening. There's a rhythm to a street and there's a rhythm to being close to a neighbor. You can experience it. It happens around holidays; it happens around the weekend. There are movements in the house, the lights going off and on, sounds. I used to bring flowers over to her from my garden. I have a big rose garden in the back. And I'd just drop off flowers. And she'd bring over apple cake. We still do that, but it's less accessible. Not as inaccessible as if she had moved to another city, but it's nonetheless not as easy as just across the street.

But we never had the type of relationship where we would just drop in on each other. We might drop things off, but we wouldn't stay. We would usually call each other first and check whether it would be OK to come. And I think that's out of a knowledge, probably, although I'll have to check this out with her, that we both really like our own space. And don't like to be just walked in on. But we would arrange to use each other's kitchens, for example, if I needed an extra oven or extra refrigerator space, or she would use my space for Seder and I would use her space for Thanksgiving or Christmas preparations for big holiday meals. We would ask each other when we needed extra space or extra oven space. Or we would ask if we could do anything to help during that time. There was a lot of sharing. And then when we planned to do that, she would just come in and use the oven or get the stuff, but that's a different kind of thing.

So when she first moved, it was traumatic. But she kept me informed all the way along as she was looking at houses. I'd go with her to look. We did that together. And she was reassuring me, "It's not England" she'd start out with, "And it's not out of state, it's right in the neighborhood." And we'd go and look and see the house. It was traumatic for both of us. For her to leave the neighborhood that she'd been in for twenty-some years. And for me to stay there. I still have feelings. I will go over and there will be a light in that house and I'll have a flashback about her being there. It's more noticeable in the summer than in the winter. And I think at times it's still traumatic. At times Gina will call me and say, "You know, if I were across the street I'd be meeting you in the street hugging right now."

But we talk to each other probably three times a week, and see each other maybe twice a week. And we send each other notes or cards, and faxes. Just to check in or to tell her that I'm thinking about her. I'll find a card that looks like something that I think she would enjoy. Or I'll see two old women sitting together on a beach or whatever and I'll write something like, "When you're in a wheelchair and I'm not, we'll still be going to the beach." Or she'll send me that kind of a card, because she sometimes has trouble with her back. And we do a lot of things together. She's a good person to do things with. I wanted to take Yoga. So I called her and asked if she wanted to. We both asked our husbands if they wanted to do it and felt that the four of us could do it, but they didn't want to, so the two of us did it. And we learned Yoga, and we do that every day. We don't do it together, but she does it and I do it and we check in with each other. But we had great, great fun.

We basically do things to just have space and time. I used to row on the river. She never did that with me, but sometimes she would come down and read while I was rowing. I remember her coming several times and sitting, and while I rowed she would watch or read or do something else. Many of the things we would learn together had to do with being centered, being able to do some sort of meditation, or some sort of way of helping us through a rough time, being together.

So it's not really a lot of time that we spend together. I was thinking about that. We usually see each other once or twice a week, talk to each other on the phone occasionally, not long conversations usually, unless something is happening that we need to check out with each other and talk about. But it's usually just a glimpse, or a passing, "Hello, what's happening? How are you? I was thinking about you. How are things going?"

As Deb and Gina enter each new phase of their lives, Deb clearly treasures her fortune in having someone to travel down those paths with her:

We've talked about what it's like for us as we go through new stages in our life. I'm halfway through menopause, so we talk about that a lot. Wanting different things from our sexual partners. Wanting to be maybe left alone. She'll talk about how her husband's always talking about what she wears to bed. My husband does that too. And we'll say that to our husbands: "Get off my back about wearing big, long, flannel nightgowns." And when we were younger married people we used to not wear anything to bed and now we get cold so we wear things to bed. And my husband likes to hug me when he's falling asleep, while I can't fall asleep now with him hugging me. When we talk about those things to each other, it encourages us to talk to our husbands about them more directly.

Lately I've been starting to think, and we've talked about it a little bit, about what it will be like to be getting into old age and thinking about dying. Thinking about our partners dying. We kid about who's going to go first, or this wheelchair thing again. I've often said to her, if somebody's going to lock me up for mental reasons don't let them do it. Part of it's funny, but part of it's not. She has a mom who's been locked up. Not locked up, but she's gotten electroshock treatments for depression, and I think sometimes when she goes through things with her mother she worries about herself and how she'll be, as she ages. And so we talk about keeping each other clued in on that and advocating for each other. Say somebody would say, "Well, I think you ought to go away or be put away," you need somebody there to say, "Well, no, I don't think so" or "That wouldn't be her wishes; I would fight for her." I worry that Bob would just be distraught and would tend more to give in to what the doctors would say about what should be done. He tends to listen more to authority figures. He would be more likely to give in if they are telling him that this would be for the best. While Gina would be more focused on what she knows I would want.

And I've also more recently started to think about what it would be like if she weren't in my life. I think it would be very hard. . . . I'm tearing up. It's interesting, we've both said that to each other, written it in birthday cards to our mothers, and talked it over with our husbands. In fact, Jimmy said a funny thing to Gina. He said, "Well, would you want to leave any money to Deb?" It wasn't quite that glib, but it was kind of sweet, I thought. So our husbands have been grateful for our relationship.

I think the reason I think of Gina as my best friend is that she's a combination of things I need to have in my life. I really can't imagine not being able to check in or tell her what's going on. If something comes up or if some good thing or problematic thing happens, I can't imagine not being able to talk to her. And I can imagine that if she were to die before me that I would talk to her. I would continue to talk to her. I mean I . . . I'm going to cry now. Gina and I have talked about . . . talking to ourselves. I do that a lot. I talk to myself and answer myself. (Now you know why I don't want electroshock therapy.) But she's shared with me that she does that too. So, I think it's one of the illustrations of how there's an ability to share something that's relatively small. It's not a big, earth-shattering thing. But being able to talk to somebody who's my same age, and it doesn't quite feel as lonely, or it doesn't feel strange, or it doesn't feel weird. Or, it might feel weird—in fact, she might say, "It's so weird that I do that and that you do that." And yet there's something, not exactly leveling, but it's like a peer, it's like somebody who's there at the same time with you.

Everybody who knows me knows what Gina means to me. I'm starting to cry again . . . I think because I don't often talk at length about what she means to me. I mean literally explaining why she is my best friend. So I think I'm getting—I think it means a lot to me. She means a lot to me. And having her to talk to about significant things, about crazy things, about things I do that—I don't know. . . . She's my best friend because we've been through a lot together. We've kept each other informed about what's really going on while we're going through a lot. And it's one of the rare relationships in life that isn't pseudo. I don't feel like I have to make up something in order to be with Gina. I can just be. And that's rare. It's a gift. So that's why she's my best friend.

FURTHER REFLECTIONS:
A DIFFERENT KIND OF FRIENDSHIP

Although each of the participants' stories is unique, Deb's is continually striking to me for the number of things she brings up about her friendship that none of the other participants allude to. Three in particular stand out: that her friendship with Gina has helped her to work on other relationships; that she talks about advocating within the relationship; and that their respective husbands have not been altogether supportive of the friendship.

Deb mentions on several occasions that she feels that her friendship with Gina has had a positive impact on relationships with other people in her life. For example, she says that although she has been concerned at times that she has used Gina as a substitute in some ways for the relationship she does not have with her sister, she also believes that her friendship with Gina has served as a model for how two women can relate to each other and has thus allowed her to try to build the relationship with her sister that she would like to have. She says that the trips she has taken with Gina encouraged her to try taking one with her sister, "which was wonderful." Deb also credits her friendship with Gina for opening up an avenue of discussion with her mother, which allowed her to gain a new perspective on her mother's feelings.

Deb believes that their friendship has had a positive impact on the way that she relates to her husband, as well. For example, she has at times used Gina as a sounding board to try out things that she would like to say to her husband. By doing that, she can hear the sound of her words and get feedback from Gina. Also, her friendship with Gina has shown her ways to be a friend in her marriage:

> The struggle for each of us in different ways has been to use our friendship skills with our husbands. And that's really been helpful. So our friendship has kind of helped us evolve a friendship with our husbands and has helped us to more easily be direct and honest with our husbands.

Thus, Deb feels that her friendship with Gina has had a positive impact on at least three other very important relationships in her life.

Deb uses the phrase "advocate for" on several occasions during the interviews. She first uses it when explaining that when they were younger, she and Gina would usually agree with each other's points of view in discussions about their respective husbands or lovers. She then goes on to explain that part of advocating for each other over the years has become trying to see the other party's side. She says that because she knows that Gina is her advocate, it usually does not bother her to have Gina try to do that. In fact, "it's really a very important role. It's a very important way for her be with me."

The other way in which she talks about each being an advocate for the other is in the context of what will happen to her if someone wants to "lock me up for mental reasons." She knows that in such a case Gina will be an advocate and not allow something to happen to her against her will. She believes that while her husband would try to do what was best for Deb, she trusts Gina to be thinking more of what Deb would want.

Deb's choice of the word advocate is noteworthy, because an advocate is someone who is more than just on your side. She is someone who actively works on your behalf. Deb thus draws a picture of a friendship that goes far beyond the more passive, but certainly significant, support of sitting together and talking about one's problems—as certainly Deb and Gina do. Deb is clear that she and Gina will jump into action whenever it is needed. From Deb's words, we get the sense that she almost expects that the day will come when she will be unable to speak for herself and will need the person she can most count on to speak for her. She knows that Gina will fill that role.

Finally, Deb talks a great deal about the feelings her husband and Gina's husband have about the friendship. Although she contradicts herself on a few occasions when talking about this, the overall understanding I gained is that they have each had to struggle with both of their husbands to try to make them understand the importance of the friendship in their lives. In fact, the first thing Deb says in this regard is that good friendships have to be "fought for" when one is in a heterosexual relationship. She says that both of her husbands and both of Gina's did not always understand the relationship and were jealous. She explains that her current husband, particularly in the beginning of the marriage, did not understand her friendship with Gina. One of the things that she and Bob had to negotiate early in their marriage was finding time for Deb to be with Gina. Deb also says that all the husbands came to understand and even appreciate the friendship. Although Bob, and Gina's current husband, Jimmy, sometimes still feel left out, she thinks that, in many ways, they really like that Deb and Gina have the relationship they do.

Her final words on the subject, however, are not quite so rosy. In our final interview, I ask Deb whether there have been issues within the friendship surrounding competitiveness. She says that there are never competitive feelings between Gina and her, but that both of their husbands feel competitive with the respective friend. She says that there continues to be a constant struggle with their husbands over the subject of the friendship. She explains that the issue of why they need to see each other so often is continually raised. Thus, I was left with the final impression that Deb's beliefs about how each of their husbands feel about the friendship changes according to what is going on at the time of each of the interviews. At the time of the final interview, it is clear that Deb feels once again that her friendship with Gina needs to be fought for.

Chapter 10

Denise

Denise is a twenty-two-year-old African-American woman, recently graduated from college and currently enrolled in a doctoral program. She is engaged to be married. Our two interviews took place in two separate rooms where she works. We conducted the first in a conference-sized room, in which we sat at a round table that could seat about six people. For the second interview we were in a very small room, sitting at a small rectangular table, large enough only for two.

Denise often gave short, quick answers to my questions. During the interviews, it felt to me as though she was not always giving much thought to her answers. There were also several times when she said that she did not know how she felt about something that had occurred or what her motivations had been for something she had done. Although I wondered and worried whether she felt uncomfortable during the interviews, I was also frustrated at times by what I viewed as a lack of introspection and possibly interest. At the end of the second interview, I asked her why she had chosen to become a participant. She replied that being a doctoral student, herself, she understood how difficult it can be to get participants and she wanted to help me out. I wondered if perhaps Denise came into the interviews with a preconceived notion of what their structure would be, based more on a quantitative model. Perhaps she thought that I would have a long list of questions that required fairly short answers.

After many discussions with my support group and memos to myself about my frustrations with Denise, I came to realize that a large part of the difficulty was that she challenged my conception of how a woman should be, both within her friendships and as an interviewee. That is, I expected that like my woman friends and me, the women in my study would have thought a great deal about their friendships and about their feelings, and that they would want to talk at length about them. One member of my support group asked me if I would be as frustrated if a man did not seem particularly introspective—and I realized that I would not. I clearly had expectations for women in this area. But then I also had to wonder whether it made sense to include Denise in my study, if she did not have all that much to say about her friendships. I realized, however, that she had plenty to say. I just had to allow myself to hear it.

THE STORY

Patti

In setting the scene of her early friendship with Patti, Denise brings us back in time—not just in her life, but for those of us who had a childhood best friend, in ours. In a few short sentences, Denise elicits feelings of pleasure and contentment in me, as I recollect the hours on end my best friend and I would spend in one or the other's bedroom just playing and talking:

> Patti and I grew up in the same neighborhood. We were two when we met. Our parents knew each other and we went to school together, off and on, until high school. She's six months younger than I am, and one grade behind me. But even when we didn't go to school together, we were still friends. We did everything together as children, and whenever I go home, we still go out and do stuff together, and we talk on the phone a lot.
>
> When we were children we would play all day, just the two of us, just by ourselves. There were other people in our neighborhood, other children that we would play with sometimes. But there were times when we would go into my basement or into her basement and just play. We would play Barbie dolls or take on characters of different people and pretend that we were somebody else, or whatever. Whenever we spent the night at each other's houses, we would play like we were roommates in a hospital. We'd make up all kinds of illnesses.
>
> When I think about Patti, I think about her as more than a best friend. We've talked about how we think our relationship has surpassed friendship. It's like we're family. We used to tell people we were cousins. But also when I think about who's really my best friend, it's my mom. I feel closest to her. And I talk to her about everything. But she's family. Patti is my closest friend outside my family.

Few would argue that part of being in a close friendship is seeing one's friend through crises. It is noteworthy that the youngest of my participants is the one whose friendship was most affected by such an event:

In junior high school, Patti got cancer. It was really weird because it was my fourteenth birthday party, during the summer before I went to the ninth grade, and we went to pick her up. We walked down the street to walk her to my house because it was dark. She was saying she didn't feel well, but she wanted to come for a little while. She had gone to the doctor that day and they told her it was nothing and sent her home. She later saw another doctor, and then she was admitted to the hospital on my birthday.

I cried a lot because I didn't understand what it meant. When you hear "cancer," as a child, you just think "fatal" immediately. But then my mom explained it to me, because I guess she had talked to Patti's mom about what was going on. She had surgery either the day she was admitted or the next day. I was at the hospital just about every day. I was there almost as much as she was. I would go to school and then after school my high school best friend and I would both go see her.

I cried a lot at first, and then again there was another period where I cried a lot because when I was in the hospital she always looked hurt. They had to take blood all the time. Before, she was like I am—scared of pain. And you can tell that she's not like that anymore. Pain doesn't bother her anymore. But I remember one time they were taking blood, and there was nothing coming out. They had exhausted the vein, and I cried the whole rest of the day. I mean it didn't bother her. They just took it from another vein, but I just kept thinking, "She's in pain," and that was what bothered me.

And then when she was on chemo, her hair fell out. It would grow back between times, and then it would fall out again. So she would wear wigs. After her last treatment, she couldn't decide if she should keep wearing wigs while her hair grew out. It was a big deal to her. And I told her—because I hated her wig—if she stopped wearing a wig, I'd cut my hair too. So I cut it. My dad couldn't believe I did it. It wasn't in to wear really short hair back then, the way it is now. The first day when I got my hair cut, her mom and she picked me up from the hairdresser and we went to the football game that night. Everybody was just looking at us like, "Oh, I can't believe she cut her hair." I mean they knew about Patti, but they couldn't believe I cut my hair. But we just kept saying, "They're looking at us because we're so beautiful." I think it helped her.

Although Denise rather matter of factly presents her decision to cut her hair, it is a touching act of generosity and kindness. Similarly, we see her love and thoughtfulness in the insight she has into Patti and the pride she seems to take in her friend:

That whole thing really changed her. She used to be really quiet and timid. She was always scared that people were going to talk about her. And I don't know why, because she was always really nice and cute. But after she was sick, she became more outgoing. In high school, she tried out to be one of the dancers that dance in front of the band at football games, and she made the squad. In the band, everyone is in the same uniform and no one can recognize you, but when you're in the front dancing you have to wear sequins, and outfits, and stuff. And it was shocking. That was her first coming out, when she started showing that she was more outgoing. She was the captain her senior year. That was also the first time I saw her leadership abilities or potential. I was always the little boss when we were younger, and I guess being away from me being as overbearing and loud as I am, she was able to be a leader. That's how she was in her sorority, too. She didn't hold an office, but she coordinated a lot of the events and stuff like that.

While other participants talk about the difficulty inherent in maintaining emotional closeness across physical distance, Denise does not describe any such problems in her relationship with Patti, perhaps in part because of the acceptance each has for the other and for the disparate paths taken:

When I first went to college, I thought it would be difficult to leave all my friends. Patti went to school back home. But I made new friends and I still saw Patti and talked to her on the phone. She would come to visit me a lot and would come down for special events and stuff. And then I would come back home too. I came for her graduation from high school. Then when she went to college— she's a year behind me in school—I would stay with her on campus some weekends and she would come and stay with me sometimes. And we would always just go out with each other's friends. I always got along with her friends, and she always got along with mine. Well, actually that's not true. She had one friend in high school—I wouldn't consider her one of her best friends—but it was one of her friends she'd hang out with a lot. And she didn't like me at all. I don't know why. And it wasn't until about a year ago that she finally decided that we could get along. But she never wanted to go somewhere if I was coming along. Patti would just say, "I don't know why y'all don't get along." Patti's really sweet and she just always wants peace. She always wants everybody to be nice to each other and stuff. So we just resolved the conflict by not being around each other. It didn't really cause any problems, because Patti and I didn't hang out much while we were in high school.

Now we talk on the phone a lot. I write to her, but she doesn't really write back. She's just busy, and there are some people that just don't sit down and take the time to write. But I don't think anything about it. I just know she doesn't write; I always knew that. I write just to say hi. Because she still lives with her parents, and I know when we were kids we used to like to receive mail. So I just do it so she can get mail. It's just nice to get something in the mail, because when you live with your parents, the majority of the mail is your parents'. So I just send her a card or something. A letter, a note, whatever.

Patti and I talk a lot, too. Just about what's going on with her. Like she was looking for a job for a long time and couldn't find one. Or about how she's looking forward to moving out of her parents' house. And she has a boyfriend she's been with for awhile. Just whatever. Oh, and about my wedding. Both she and Mary are going to be in my wedding. So we talk about what everyone's going to wear. It's hard to find a dress that complements everybody's figure. And she and Mary and my mom are working together to get stuff done.

Patti and I can go to each other with anything. I feel that way, and she tells me a lot. With her parents being so protective, there are a lot of things her parents never talk to her about—specifically about men and sex and stuff. And so we always talked about it or I would tell her whatever my mom said to me. Or she would talk to my mom. I guess that helped us talk about other things, too. I mean if you can get past that you can basically talk about anything.

The picture of the friendship becomes more complete as we learn what Patti gives to Denise:

Patti's very supportive. When I decided to go to grad school, it wasn't a big deal to my family. It was almost like the next step. When you graduate from high school, you go to college, and when you graduate from college, you go to grad school. But when I decided to go to grad school and not come back home, some of my other friends would say, "Why are you going to school again? Why don't you come home and stop going to school?" But Patti would say, "Well, I'll see you on holidays." She said I should go if that's what I wanted. And I was thinking about taking some time off. I told Patti that I didn't know whether I should go to school or not because I was kind of burned out on school for a period. But she said, "Well, don't go to summer school. Come home and work, and we can go out and stuff all summer, and then maybe you'll feel different about going to school." So that's what I did. I worked as a secretary for the summer. It was kind of mindless. And it helped a lot. See she knows me. She knows I'd get a job and get comfortable and not go back to school.

I really don't like being in the North right now, so I can talk to her about that a lot. She just listens. I mean there's really nothing anybody can say or do about me not liking this place, but sometimes she'll say things like, "Well, you can always come home for break." It helps just to talk about it, just to tell somebody how much I hate it. Every time I talk about it here, everybody says, "Oh, it's such a wonderful city and there's so much to do." And I just keep thinking it's dirty and cold. When I describe it to her, she understands. She's never been here, but she's still in the South, so I can tell her. Once I called her and it was seventy degrees there and it was twenty here. And she teased me. She said, "I'm going out to play tennis."

Mary

When Denise went to high school, she and Patti were no longer in school together. As is often the case in childhood, Denise developed another best friendship in this separate environment—just as kids may have a camp best friend and a school best friend:

Mary and I didn't start going to school together until the seventh grade, when I came into the magnet school system. Mary, Patti, and I were in the same carpool. And then Mary and I went to high school together—Patti didn't come to our high school—so I guess that's how we became best friends. She's more my best friend from high school. She lives in the same neighborhood as us—she lives next door to Patti—but she moved in later. When we were children, we played together a lot. There was another girl, Marsha, who was the same age as Patti, and the four of us would play spades and gin all the time. They used to call us the four old women, because we played cards all the time. Mary and I usually got along, but we were both very outspoken and always wanting to be the boss. So we had conflicts.

Just as Denise's friendship with Patti gives us a glimpse of young friends dealing with traumatic circumstances, her friendship with Denise provides a look at a teenage friendship placed under the strain of significant social pressures:

We were friends all through high school, but we had a falling out one time. We went to a school that was predominantly white. There were only a few black people in the school. And we pretty much hung out together. But I also had some white friends. And Mary didn't. She and a lot of the other black girls would say things about me, like I thought I was better than them, or they'd always ask me why I wanted to hang out with the white people. And then we had to do our family trees in English class. I have a lot of native American and white on both sides of my family. And my family tree, the one my grandmother does, has everybody's ethnicity in there also. When I brought that tree in, they said things like, "You're trying to prove that you're white. You're trying to tell everybody that you're white." That went on for about a month. Finally I just got really mad. See, at first I was just ignoring it, and then I got really mad. We fell out. And then it was over. I told them that I couldn't help what was in my family tree, and that it doesn't matter who my friends are. That I don't have to be with them all the time. It was hard, but we worked it out . . . we had to, basically. I guess we didn't have to stay friends, but we felt we needed to stay friends because there were so few blacks in the school, so we tried.

As they entered their college years, Denise and Mary grew closer, and as inevitably happens as intimacy increases, some conflicting feelings came to the surface:

Mary and I went to college near each other, but we didn't see each other that often. We saw each other more at home. And she left school after first semester sophomore year. She moved back home because her parents couldn't afford to send her anymore. I guess we became really close then. I don't know why, I have no clue. She started talking to me more, and whenever she was having problems at home, she would call me and tell me about it. I guess she felt like she could talk to me. She started telling me more about the problems her family was having. Like her parents, they're still married, but they may as well not be married. They still live in the same house, but that's about it. It was bothering her, but she didn't talk about it until she had to come back home from school. That's when she started talking about things that were going on at her house.

But she had problems with them before she started talking to me about it. I could just tell. She never wanted to be at home. She would stay up at my house. Or if we went out she would stay out as late as possible, and then go to sleep and get up and leave in the morning. I never asked her about it, though. I waited until she wanted to talk to me about it.

Mary also has really poor taste in men. For a long time she was in a really bad relationship. She would always call me and talk about all the bad things that were going on, which sometimes bothered me because she knew that it was bad, but she was staying anyway. That was a conflict, because I couldn't tell her what I really felt. I wanted to just tell her that she was being stupid—just to leave him alone. But I didn't want to hurt her feelings about it. She knew I didn't like the guy. She would tell him, "Denise doesn't like you." And I would say things like, "Why are you complaining and still in the relationship? You could do better." But after awhile she wasn't listening to me, so I just didn't say anything.

When she was first getting out of that relationship, she would always say stuff about my fiancé like, "I wish I could have somebody like Timmy." And she'll say, "Does Timmy have a brother?" You know, she'll say silly things like that, but I don't know, I try not to read into it too much. I don't want to think that she's jealous of me. But sometimes it seems that way.

Denise clearly greatly values her relationship with Mary, but she recognizes that there are areas of difficulty and imbalance:

Mary's always there whenever I need her, but I guess I feel like she needs me more than I need her. I feel lucky that everything's going well for me, but sometimes I feel bad talking to her, because she does have so many problems. Like when I got my fellowship to come up here, at first I didn't want to tell her, because I thought it would make her feel bad. But she seemed happy about it. But I don't know how she really feels about my being in school. I don't really talk about school. She'll ask me, "How's school going?" and I'll say it's going fine or something like that, but we don't usually talk about school. I don't want to make her feel bad.

I do talk to her about stuff like whenever Timmy and I fall out. And I also talk to her about not liking it up here. But she thinks I should just move home. She says, "Well you could go to school here. Just move home." But I don't think she really understands. I mean she understands that the reason I chose to come here is because Timmy was up here and that I got money to come here to go to school, and that I'm going to stay here until I finish. But she thinks I could just leave and come home. And she'll have plans. She'll say, "You don't have to live at home. We can get an apartment together." Stuff like that.

Sometimes, with Mary, I feel like what I have to talk about is petty, because I don't have any problems at home. I feel like my family's perfect. Well, that's what everybody says about us. We have our flaws, but we get along for the most part. Mary always calls my family the Cosby family and stuff like that. She says that a lot. She'll say, "You're family's perfect." She was at our house one day, and my mom was in the kitchen, and my dad kept going up behind her and kissing her and stuff, and grabbing her and pulling her away. Or she helped me throw my parents' twenty-fifth wedding anniversary party, and she would say, "Your family's just too perfect."

Mary's close to my mom, too. They work together at the mall, when my mom isn't teaching. They usually try to fix their schedule so they're together. I know Mary talks about things that are going on with her. And sometimes they talk about me. They'll discuss me in my absence. I tell them pretty much the same things, so that's fine with me. Sometimes they can come up with solutions. Sometimes I get a little jealous, though, because I can't be with my mom and she can. I thought about that a lot when I first came up here. But I know that I can share my mother. It doesn't bother me anymore.

I don't really know why I call Mary a best friend. I know if I have a problem I'll call her before some of my other friends, or if I just want to tell her something good happened. I remember she started calling me her best friend first, and I guess I just started because she did. I mean I do feel like we have a special friendship, aside from other friends that I have.

FURTHER REFLECTIONS:
ARE ALL BEST FRIENDS CONSIDERED EQUAL?

All of the five participants who talk about having two best friends seem to feel closer to or more intimate with one than the other. With Denise, however, the disparity seems particularly marked. Whereas Denise's relationship with Patti is so close that they have talked about how it "surpasses" friendship, there are facets of her friendship with Mary that made it difficult for me to conceptualize the relationship as a best friendship.

Denise talks about how important it is to her to be able to call Patti and talk to her about not liking her living situation. She says that Patti is the only person she can really talk to about that because she understands that Denise needs her to listen and perhaps offer some words of support. Patti knows that Denise is not looking for a solution. In contrast, when she tells Mary how she feels, Mary suggests that Denise come back home to finish school. Thus, whereas Patti understands that Denise needs to stay, both to finish her degree and to be with her fiancé, Mary does not. Further, Mary seems to be thinking about how nice it would be for *her* if Denise came home and they could live together.

Similarly, Denise says that when she was thinking about whether she should go immediately on to graduate school or take a year off, Patti understood that the best thing for Denise would be to come home for the summer but then to continue her studies. In contrast, some of Denise's other friends said things like, "Why are you going to school again? Why don't you come home and stop going to school?" Although it is not clear if Mary is among the latter group, Denise does not say that she, like Patti, was supportive about Denise leaving and going on in school.

Also, Denise explains that she does not always tell Mary everything, because she does not want to "make her feel bad." Denise sometimes hesitates to tell Mary about problems she is having because they feel "petty" in comparison to Mary's problems. On the flip side, when Denise got her fellowship she was also hesitant to share her joy with Mary. Denise also expresses some concern that Mary might feel jealous of her because Mary has expressed a desire for someone in her life like Timmy. Denise seems to expend a fair amount of conscious energy avoiding subjects relevant to her own life that could potentially hurt Mary.

Near the end of the first interview, I ask Denise why she thinks she calls Mary a best friend. This follows from her telling me that she and Patti recently had a conversation about the nature of their friendship and how they feel as if they are "beyond best friends." She explains that the best friendship label originated with Mary. Denise never articulates any further than that why she considers Mary a best friend.

For some time, I wondered if in fact Denise labeled the friendship a best friendship solely because Mary had done so. Since Denise does not seem to be able to be honest with Mary on a variety of levels, and Mary does not seem to understand Denise in the way that Patti does, it seemed to me that perhaps Denise would not consider Mary a best friend if she did not feel the need to reciprocate Mary's feelings about her. Therefore, it did not seem to me to be a *true* best friendship.

I came to see, however, that my reasoning was not sound on two levels. First, there is clearly no right or wrong way for someone to come to label a friend as a best friend. Thus, Mary is no less a best friend because I have difficulty understanding the means through which Denise came to that definition. The second level derives from the overall difficulty I had in relating to Denise, largely because she does not tend to be introspective. When Denise says that she does not know why she calls Mary her best friend, that does not mean that there was no reason. It means, rather, that Denise does not know what the reason was. And further, when I probe deeper and ask her what makes their friendship special, she does have some answers:

D: I know if I have a problem I'll call her. Or if I just want to tell her something good that happened, I'll call her before some of my other friends. I mean I like being around her more. And I'm speaking of other friends, not Patti.

P: I'm just probing, so forgive me if I keep asking the same thing. What is it about either her or your relationship with her or your feelings about her that would prompt you to call her, rather than some of your other friends, a best friend?

D: I just feel comfortable talking to her. I know that she wouldn't say anything to anybody else about what we talk about.

My initial biases did not allow me to see these aspects of their friendship as sufficient for it to be labeled by Denise as a best friendship. It seemed to me that because Denise was not digging deeper, she did not see that Mary was not *really* a best friend. But I came to understand that the aspects of their friendship she does articulate are what set it off from Denise's other friendships, excluding that with Patti. Thus, although I think that Denise would agree that the feelings she has for Patti are different from those for Mary, she would also say—as she did by including that friendship in the study—that Mary is definitely a best friend.

Chapter 11

"They're Both People Who Truly Know Me": A Need Fulfilled

In quantitative analysis, if a finding is present across virtually all cases—or participants—it is said to be highly statistically significant. If I may be so bold as to co-opt that concept here, omitting the word "statistically"—for I know that my more quantitative-minded peers would pounce on any hint on my part to link my methodology to the conclusions one may purportedly draw from a more "scientific" methodology—the feeling of being known among women best friends is just such a finding. All of the participants in the study said they felt known by their best friends. Virtually all said that their best friend or friends knew them in a way few, if any, others did. The experience of being deeply known goes to the heart of their best friendships. It is a defining characteristic of these relationships.

Unfortunately, I made the mistake early in my analysis of equating near universality with simplicity. I originally failed to see the complexity inherent in such a powerful finding, when in fact, that very power made it a tremendously difficult concept to wrestle into a shape that worked for me. In its strength, it refused to allow me to find a tidy way to conceptualize and write about it. (If anthropomorphizing a concept is the only somewhat emotionally disturbed thing you do while you are immersed in the depths of research, you are in good shape.) It continually fought with me to see it for more than I was seeing it. And I, in my stubbornness, fought back, because as is a pitfall with all kinds of research, I was sure I already knew what this theme was about. I, myself, have felt known at times and not known at others—often by the same friend. My experience, I was sure, was clearly the same as my participants'. But what makes qualitative research so wonderful when it is practiced with care is that the researcher is forced to listen closely to her participants' words. We cannot entirely silence the voices in our heads, but we can find ways to temporarily mute them, or at least turn the volume way down. Few things are as intellectually satisfying as reaching a new level of understanding by finding a way to see things in the data that for whatever reason are very difficult for one, personally, to see.

It is for these reasons that the reader will find this chapter organized differently from the other two theme chapters. "Knowing"—as I came to call this intractable theme—and I came to a compromise, of sorts. It would allow me to find a way to conceptualize it so that I could make a coherent presentation, and I would acknowledge its enormous significance. I got the better part of the bargain—the role of knowing in women's friendships is evident in one way or another, with no additional help from me, on virtually every page of this book. It was unavoidable.

Four overarching dimensions of knowing emerged among the data. The first involves the length of the friendship. The participants who talk about this aspect of knowing explain that their friends have known them through different periods of their lives and have seen them change and grow. The second dimension revolves around the women's beliefs that their friends are attuned to them in such a way that they can see below the facade they may be presented with. The third dimension of knowing is that of understanding. Many of the women talk about understanding as a deeper form of knowing, so that there are those who may know them but not understand them. Finally there is the aspect of knowing that enables the women's friends to offer words of advice based on their knowledge of their friend. I also include a separate section focusing solely on Deb, because, alas, in the end "Knowing" refused to submit entirely to my tidy categories and forced me to acknowledge the pores in their borders. Indeed, Deb's own construction of this theme demands special treatment.

"THEY'VE SEEN ME THROUGH A LOT OF CHANGES"

Amy brings up the idea of knowing early in the first interview. In response to my asking her how she would compare her relationship with Janine to other relationships in her life, outside of that with Nina, Amy says:

> My relationships with Nina and Janine are very similar to my relationship with my husband, in that they know me well and in that we've got some years behind us. And so we've seen each other grow over the years.

For Amy, this idea that her friends have seen her grow and change over a period of years appears to be central to why she considers these relationships best friendships. Janine and Nina knew Amy before she was a Christian and shared the experience of her becoming a Christian with her. Thus, they know her in a way that most others cannot. Although Amy makes clear throughout the interview that she feels very close to her husband, and in fact considers him her best friend, this is an area in which he just cannot know her as well as Nina and Janine do:

> [H]e and I met at the end of my time at college, and because my four years at college were a really formative time for me—that's when I became a Christian and a lot of things changed for me— he didn't get to see that. Nina and Janine were there at the time.

Amy reiterates in the second interview the importance to her that Nina and Janine have known her "from the beginning." She does so when explaining to me that it had occurred to her following the first interview that she had not talked about her friend Barb. She is somewhat surprised by this omission, because Barb is someone who, until she moved, Amy saw and talked to on a far more regular basis than she did either Nina or Janine. Although Amy feels very close to Barb and has much in common with her, "the immediacy of that friendship, I guess, wasn't salient enough for me to have talked about Barb, primarily." This discussion leads me to ask Amy how she labels friends—how she thinks she came to conclude that Nina and Janine are her best friends. Amy explains that Barb has not been a witness to Amy's growth over time. For that reason, Amy feels that Barb does not know her in the same way as her other two friends know her.

Nancy also talks about the fact that her friends have had the opportunity to see her change and grow over time, as well as seeing her through difficult and significant periods of her life. As a result, they know her in ways newer friends cannot:

A piece of it is life experience and critical life experiences that you have with certain people. Claudia was my friend since my first year of college, and we just have been through a lot together.

Later, when talking about how both Claudia and Lisa know her in ways others do not, Nancy says that they have "known me through different times."

Deb, as she so often does, talks about a process that involves her and Gina together. Thus, unlike Amy and Nancy, who say that their friends have seen them change and grow, Deb talks about how she and Gina have grown up together. When I ask her if she can compare her relationship with Gina with other friendships she has, she says:

I have some other good friends, mostly that I've gotten through my work, my writing, or my schooling. The biggest difference I would say is that this is over such a long period of time. It's like we've grown up together. I'd say that's the biggest difference.

Finally, Alice and Liz both echo the sentiments of the other participants. Alice, in talking about the roles Julia plays in her life, says that it is important to her to be "able to talk to somebody who I know knows me for a long time, and through a lot of different changes." Liz, talking about Sandy, mentions that Sandy knows things about her that others do not: "We went to high school together, so she *really* knows all the nitty-gritty stuff, like way back to my first boyfriend— in ninth grade." Although Liz feels that her two friends know her equally, clearly an element of Sandy's knowing is that she knew her "way back when," as well as in the intervening years.

"THEY'RE VERY ATTUNED TO MY FEELINGS"

Toward the end of the second interview, I ask Nancy how her two best friendships are similar and different. She tells me that "they're both people who, friendshipwise, I think truly know me." When I ask her what she thinks knowing means, she initially struggles:

What do I think knowing me means? I don't know, I think . . . that they, I don't know, I think they just *know* me. They know . . . they have a good sense of when I'm with them. I think they're very attuned to my feelings. I probably have to say less than I have to say to other people. They wouldn't miss my being hurt or being tense about something. They would pick it up. I think that they're pretty on target about what interests me, and both of them could engage me probably very quickly. Most often, I'll engage very quickly with people, but if I'll be less in a mood, both of them easily could engage me. It's hard to say. It's not a superficial relationship.

She then brings up Laura, another friend, as a person to compare with Lisa and Claudia. She tells of an incident in which Laura has been extraordinarily giving with her time. She says that Laura is really there for her and is someone she can "always count on." But although that, too, is a significant aspect of best friendship for Nancy, Laura is not a best friend:

> Even though I see Laura all the time, my friendship with her is not as deep as it is with Claudia and Lisa. We're less attuned to each other. Like if I'm in a bad mood, there could be this huge distance between us that is going to be very hard for either one of us to figure out how to cross, where that's not true with a friend you're closer with.

That attunement must exist for Nancy to define a friendship as a best friendship. This aspect of knowing is particularly important to her because she recognizes that she is not an easy person to get to know. She understands that truly knowing her requires breaking down barriers that she has constructed. She feels that only Claudia and Lisa have accomplished that.

Interestingly, Nancy is aware that Claudia feels that she does not know Nancy as well as she would like to. Nancy says that at times Claudia pushes her to be more open, and asks her questions just to try to get her to open up. She refers to one period in which Claudia was reading a book, presumably about relationships, which led her to press Nancy even further. Claudia would "ask outrageous questions" in an effort to get Nancy to be more open.

In my second interview with Amy, after she has told me about how her friendship with Barb differs from those with Nina and Janine, I ask her what she thinks it means that Nina and Janine know her. After a bit of thought, she tells me about the conversation in which Janine had been able to see that Amy was avoiding something. She says that she thinks knowing is "understanding without having to be told, or without having to explain." When I ask her how it made her feel that Janine could read her that well, she responds:

> Actually it felt great to know that we had a close enough relationship, and that she knew me well enough, to know that I couldn't get away with stuff like that. Whereas some of my friends, if it was the same interaction, I'm sure they wouldn't have picked up anything and I could have just gone on and wouldn't have been confronted at all. And maybe that would have been more comfortable, but it was better for her to have confronted me on it. So it felt good.

Thus, like Nancy, Amy appreciates that her friends can see through her defenses. Although she knows it might be more comfortable for her in the moment if she had been allowed to avoid acknowledging her true feelings, in the long run she is glad to have people in her life who will not let her do so. These sentiments echo something Amy talks about in the first interview when she is discussing Nina as a friend. She explains that Nina tends to be more up-front than Janine in her opinions and will tell Amy if she does not agree with something that Amy is doing or intends to do. When I ask her how she feels about that, she replies:

> I think when it comes from her it's very welcome, because I know that she's really tried to understand the situation before she says, "That sounds nuts." And so I appreciate that perspective, to hear from someone who I think knows me, who I know cares about me, and who seems to understand the situation— that I'm being nuts or whatever.

Thus, when criticism is offered by someone who cares about her *and* who knows her, she gratefully accepts it.

Finally, Liz, Denise, and Alice also say that their best friends are able to read them in a way that most others cannot. When I ask Liz what she thinks knowing is and how she thinks it develops, she explains that words are not always necessary for her friends to be able to understand what is going on with her: "I think they're able to read me pretty well, so that they can tell when I'm uncomfortable or when I'm unhappy—when something's bothering me." Similarly, Denise, in response to my question about what effect the length of the relationship has on the friendship, says:

> We know each other. For instance, Mary can finish my sentences and be right. And Patti, knows if I'm in a bad mood or whatever. She can tell, even when I'm trying to play it off. She knows how to cheer me up. She just knows little things.

Thus, knowing a friend is being attuned to her moods, as well as knowing just what she is going to say. Alice, after my probing into what she means when she says that Julia is attentive, says: "She is sensitive. She's sensitive to our interactions—to what takes place. She picks up on feelings. She hears how I'm feeling, even if I'm not saying it."

"THEY DON'T JUST KNOW ME, THEY UNDERSTAND ME"

Liz draws a clear distinction between knowing and understanding. I ask Liz if her fiancé, Jeff, "knows you as well or more than Susan and Sandy do?" She replies that "he knows me like a book" and that he can tell "the minute I'm unhappy." But she goes on to say that Jeff is not as sensitive as either Susan or Sandy and, therefore, does not always *understand* her. When I ask her what the difference is between knowing and understanding, she says:

> Well, if a topic comes up and I'm uncomfortable or something, Jeff will immediately pick up on it, as will Sandy and Susan. But I don't think Jeff will fully understand why that makes me feel uncomfortable to the extent that Sandy and Susan do, even though we can all sit down and talk about it. If I had the conversation with Susan, with Sandy, and with Jeff, separately, those two would have a much better understanding than Jeff would.

I then ask her why she thinks it is that her friends understand her better than her fiancé does. She says that she thinks it is in part that her friends are women and thus have an understanding of her that Jeff cannot have, and in part that they know a little bit more about her past than Jeff does: "I mean they know some things that I've done that Jeff doesn't know about, things that have had a pretty big influence on me." Also, she thinks that it is just a matter of Jeff's personality—that "he's pretty much a straight shooter, so he's very analytical, and a lot of times my feelings don't fit into those categories." She also relates a recent illustrative anecdote: She and Jeff had gone to a party made up of Jeff's friends. At some point Jeff wanted to leave and go get beer and Liz wanted to go with him. He thought it was ridiculous for her to come with him, and she was angry that he wanted to leave her at a party where she did not feel comfortable. She felt that Jeff simply could not understand her point of view. When she told Sandy about the incident, however, Sandy expressed that she thought that Jeff was completely in the wrong. Thus, Liz felt understood by Sandy, but not by Jeff.

Amy, too, talks about how her best friends understand her on a level that others cannot. A significant aspect of Amy's life that her best friends know is that she was sexually violated. The knowing of this is more than just having the knowledge. Amy feels that others can know that she has had this experience, but they cannot understand in the way that Nina and Janine do, because these two friends have had similar experiences. This presents a problem—and an obstacle— for Amy in her friendship with Barb, because she has not yet found a way to tell Barb about what happened to her. As a result, Amy feels that Barb is missing a significant link that would help her to understand Amy better. However, Amy has been wary of telling Barb, because she feels that Barb, never having had a similar experience, cannot truly understand. Thus, Amy feels that Barb can never know her in the way that Janine and Nina do.

For Amy, as for Liz, there is a qualitative difference between knowing and understanding. Amy can—and expects she will—one day tell Barb about her past, but she feels sure that Barb can never truly understand. Similarly, Jeff may know Liz well enough even to have predicted that his actions would make her angry, but Liz believes he does not fully understand why they do.

At another point in the interviews, Amy talks about the significance to her that her friends are women. As with Liz, she believes that because her friends are women—and specifically women who have experienced continual overt objectification by men—they have an ability to relate to her, and to understand her, that her husband cannot have. For Amy, understanding also comes from an ability to empathize on a very basic, yet deep, level. I think it is likely, however, that Amy would say that there are things that her husband understands about her that no one else does.

Denise, too, talks about understanding, and even distinguishes between her two best friends along this dimension. Denise tells me she does not like living in Boston and that the only one to whom she feels she can talk freely about this is Patti. Patti understands both because Denise and she are from the same place and because she can empathize with Denise. Further, she knows Denise well enough to make Denise laugh about how much better she, Patti, has it. Also, Patti has the ability to offer words of solace—again, I think, because she understands Denise. Another level of Patti's understanding is revealed later when Denise contrasts Patti's words to Mary's on the subject of Denise's unhappiness about living in a city. Mary does not understand why it is important to Denise to stay in Boston. Unlike Patti, she cannot seem to hear that Denise just needs an understanding ear.

"SHE KNOWS WHAT WOULD HAPPEN IF I DID THAT"

After explaining to me that knowing her means being able to "read her," Liz goes on to say that she also thinks that because her friends know her, they are able to provide her with advice, taking into account both their knowledge of her history and their knowledge of her as a person. Liz uses her friends as a sounding board and turns to them for help. She appreciates that they will provide that advice in a context of an understanding of who she is. She also feels that her friends really know her limits and her boundaries. Thus, they "know the proper level of intervention" and they "push my buttons and challenge me when I'm doing something questionable, but they also know when to back off and when to just say, 'this is the way it is.'"

Denise brings up this dimension of knowing when talking about how Patti helped her decide what to do about going straight from college to graduate school. Patti gave her practical advice, taking into account her knowledge about Denise:

P: So in saying that to you, what was she—she was kind of trying to find a way for you to—?

D: Yeah, to be able to go to school and not stop, because she knows
me. She knows I'd get a job, and get comfortable, and not go back
to school—

P: Oh, I see. So she was afraid you wouldn't go back?

D: Yes. If I stopped.

Denise believes that Patti gave her sage advice because she knew
her: Patti knew both that Denise would not go back to school once she
got a job, and, it seems, that the best thing for Denise *would be* to go
on to graduate school.

Amy says that in the beginning of her marriage, she used to turn to
Janine for advice about marital issues. Janine got married before
Amy and for some time was Amy's only close friend who was married. She says that Janine offered her reassurance about things that
were going on in her marriage and answered "basic questions." Amy
felt that she could go to Janine with her concerns because "we were
similar in a lot of ways and she knew who I was and had some understanding of who my husband was, and she'd gone through it." When I
ask her some time later if she ever talks to her two friends about her
sexual relationship with her husband, she says:

> With Janine I have, and I think that was part of the initial ques-
> tioning I had when we first got married. I share mostly general
> things that are problematic, that relate to other things that she
> knows about me—aspects of my personality, or my history, or
> whatever.

Thus, Amy feels she can turn to Janine both because Janine's experience is similar to her own and because Janine knows and understands her in ways others do not.

DEB

Interestingly, nowhere in my transcripts of the portions of my first
two interviews with Deb that were recorded, nor among my notes of
the remaining portions of the first two interviews, did Deb say that
Gina knew her. I found this absence striking as I began to work on this
theme, because I felt sure that Deb would say that indeed Gina did
know her—better, in fact, than anyone else did. I also found it odd

that I did not bring up the subject of knowing with her, as I had with Linda, who also had not mentioned it on her own. I think I failed to do so because it felt redundant: I had no doubt that Deb felt known by Gina. But this certainty of Deb's feelings was a warning flag for me—a moment to reflect on how my biases were affecting my research. A large part of the reason I was so sure of Deb's feelings was that being known had become a defining factor for me of best friendship among women. All of the other participants had mentioned it, and I, too, felt its importance in my best friendships. Surely, I thought, Deb—who has an extraordinarily intimate relationship with Gina—experiences that in her friendship. But I also knew that I had to explore what in Deb's words made me so sure she felt known by Gina. I, thus, went back to my transcripts to look for evidence.

After examining my first interview with Deb carefully, I came up with characteristics that are related to knowing—for instance, as mentioned earlier, Deb talks about growing up with Gina. In addition, I was drawn to the part of each of the first two interviews when Deb talks about how she and Gina had discussed advocating for each other if either of them became incapacitated in some way. She indicates that she and Gina would know each other's wishes and fight to have those wishes respected. During the interview, I am struck that Deb would choose Gina rather than her husband as an advocate. I do not follow up at that time, however, because I cannot think of a way to probe that does not sound as if I am pointing out a flaw in her relationship with her husband. I do, however, follow up on it in our next interview. This is my entry from that part of the interview:

> Deb says that she would want Gina to be an advocate for her if she were ever to be locked up. She says that she has a fear of electroshock therapy and that Gina knows that about her. I ask her how her husband fits into that equation, and she says that he would certainly be a part of it, but that she trusts Gina more to be thinking of what Deb would want. She worries that her husband would be distraught and would give in to what authority figures said about what should be done. So that if they said she should get electroshock, she worries that he would give in to that.

Thus, Deb feels that Gina not only knows her but would use that knowledge to assure that Deb's wishes were followed. Her husband may know her, too, but that knowledge may be superseded by other information he gets.

Deb mentions several times in the interviews that she wishes that Gina were there so she could check with her to see if she would agree with what Deb is saying. One of the times she expresses this sentiment, she is talking about how even when they lived across the street from each other they did not just drop in on each other unannounced. She says, "And I think that's out of a knowledge, probably, although I'll have to check this out with her, that we both really like our own space. And don't like to be just walked in on." She thinks, thus, that they had a mutual—if unspoken—understanding about respecting each other's need for space. What strikes me is that Deb's uncertainty about whether she is right seems to stem from her need for this understanding—"knowledge"—to be reciprocal. Although she may simply be saying that she knows why *she* did not do it, but would have to check with Gina to know Gina's motivations, she also seems to be intimating that their motivations must have worked in tandem—must be the same—and that she is now only surmising what they are.

In my third interview with Deb, I ask whether the idea of knowing and being known resonates for her within the context of her friendship with Gina. She replies that it does, and in response to my question as to how, she starts off by echoing to some extent what other participants have said, but then puts a new spin on it:

> She says that it resonates in the way of being able to imagine what answer Gina would give to a question or how she would feel about a situation or an activity. Or her reaction to a news item. She also says that the reverse is true. For her, the value is in that they not only assume that each of them knows, but that they check it out with each other to make sure.

I then ask her what being known means to her:

> She says that it's a product of trust. And that it is important that they both feel free enough to check it out. She says, "I don't like to feel assumed about."

Thus, Deb does not emphasize the value of being known, as the other participants do. Although she acknowledges that she is known by Gina and vice versa, what is of greatest importance to her is that

Gina and she both do not make assumptions about each other. That seems to be the aspect of knowing that she feels distinguishes her friendship with Gina from other relationships in her life.

REFLECTIONS

Knowing and being known is an extraordinarily important part of women's best friendships. Virtually all of the participants refer to it as a defining characteristic of their relationships. Interestingly, however, despite the obvious significance of this aspect of the friendships, little has been written in the friendship and relationship literature about knowing. Although there is a relatively large body of literature on self-disclosure within relationships, those works have tended to focus on the contexts in which people are most likely to disclose information to one another.[1] Rarely have the authors gone further by focusing in any depth on the meaning and nature of the knowledge that develops from self-disclosure. However, three pieces of literature that did focus on knowing have been helpful to me in understanding the nature of the phenomenon.[2]

In an article in which they described a model of intimacy in relationships, Chelune, Robison, and Kommor discussed the meaning of knowing and being known. According to the authors, mutual knowing is an integral part of intimacy: "[A]n intimate relationship is a relational process in which we come to know the innermost, subjective aspects of another, and are known in a like manner."[3] Chelune and colleagues discussed the importance of what they called metamessages and literal messages between interactants. The metamessages are the connotative aspects of what is being said, and the literal messages are the denotative aspects. With every denotative message, they claimed, there is a simultaneous metacommunication "conveyed unconsciously through nonverbal channels (e.g., tone of voice, tempo, and facial expressions)."[4] The literal messages and metamessages may well be consistent. Often, however, they are at variance with each other. If the receiver responds only to the denotative aspect, she communicates to the sender: "'I understand *what* you said (literal message), but do not know what you *mean* (metacommunication)."[5] And if the receiver responds only to the metalevel, she is not acknowledging the importance of what is being said: "It is only when the interactants transcend the ordinary communication process and can bring their metamessages to a literal level that the innermost, subjective aspects of self can truly be known."[6]

Chelune and colleagues' theory about metacommunication is supported by the participants' descriptions in the subsection on attunement. Nancy says that Lisa and Claudia "wouldn't miss my being hurt." They can see beyond and below what she presents on a superficial level. Amy says that Janine realizes that Amy is avoiding something, even though, according to Amy, "I [wasn't] doing anything to suggest that I was avoiding something." Chelune and colleagues would likely suggest that Amy was indeed doing something on an unconscious level—something that Janine knew well enough to be able to interpret. Liz, Denise, and Alice all echo the sentiments of Nancy and Amy. Their friends are clearly attending to the metamessages involved in their interactions. In addition, the participants are, in turn, acknowledging the metalevel of their own communications. Chelune and colleagues postulated that that acknowledgment by both interactants is an integral part of knowing. Without Amy's awareness that there was more to her communication than what she was verbally saying, knowing could not exist.

Chelune, Robison, and Kommor also discussed the importance of time in the development of mutual knowing within a relationship. They explained that knowledge is gained slowly both because there is so much to learn about another person and because so much of the information that will lead to the feeling of being known is very personal. The authors pointed out that the self-disclosure literature has shown that when individuals believe that a relationship may continue over a long period of time, they begin to self-disclose gradually, "beginning with impersonal and progressing to more personal information, and requiring the same amount and kind of self-disclosures, given in reciprocal fashion, from the partner. . . ."[7]

Certainly, the data from the current study support Chelune and colleagues' thesis that time is a significant component of mutual knowing in a relationship. Amy discusses at length how important it is to her that Nina and Janine have known her for so long and through so many changes. That is one of the primary distinctions she makes between her relationships with them and those with her husband and Barb. Nancy, Deb, Liz, and Alice all talk in similar terms.

Although Jordan did not focus specifically on knowing, it is clearly a significant component of what she refers to as mutual intersubjectivity, or mutuality.[8] For Jordan, mutuality involves a desire and an ability to share one's thoughts and feelings with another, as well as an interest in learning about and responding to that other person empathetically. The parties value both the process of knowing each other and participating in each other's growth. In a relationship in which there is mutuality, there is "a kind of matching intensity of involvement and interest, an investment in the exchange that is for both the self and the other. The process of relating is seen as having intrinsic value."[9] Clearly, knowing, as described by the participants, is a key component of Jordan's model.

Jordan went on to try to understand where this desire to be known has its psychological origins. Looking at the work of Daniel Stern on mother-infant relationships, she concluded that there are patterns of relatedness that could lead to individuals' later yearning to be known by another. There is, for instance, a "'self-other complementarity,' in which 'each member's actions are the complement of the partner's.'"[10] In addition, she referred to a "'mental state sharing and tuning,' in which 'there is some sense of commonality of experience or sharing of similar external or internal experience.'"[11] Jordan believed that individuals derive a pleasure from the mutuality they experience in relationships that may originate with the pleasure experienced in the interplay between mother and child. There is, according to Jordan, a clear and mutual empathic attunement from very early in the infants' lives, even if the mutuality of that attunement has an asymmetry.

Jordan also focused on female-male differences in mutuality. She believed that "[w]omen may be more attuned to shifts in feelings, while men may be more alert to behavior or ideational changes in the other."[12] These differences may speak to what both Liz and Amy feel about the differences between their friends' and their husbands' levels of understanding. Jordan noted that this gender difference means that women will more readily find a mutuality in woman-to-woman than in woman-to-man relationships. She referred specifically to a mutual empathy that often develops within woman-to-woman relationships: "Mutual empathy occurs when two people relate to each other in a context of interest in the other, emotional availability and responsiveness, and cognitive appreciation of the wholeness of the other; the intent is to understand."[13] She went on to point out that with mutual empathy, while there is an acknowledgment of the sameness between the partners, an appreciation of the differentness may be even more important. That appreciation, Jordan explained, engenders both growth in the relationship and a sense of validation for the individuals. The validation derives from feeling accepted in one's differentness. Growth then occurs as each interactant "stretches to match or understand" the other's experience. There is an excitement to all of this, as each gets to know the other and each grows individually and as part of a relationship:

> In the excitement of exploration, getting to know one another—who are you? who am I? who are we?—there is the opportunity for new self-definition; new aspects of self are expressed and each provides that opportunity for the other. This is growth through relationship.[14]

Validated seems to me an apt description of how the participants feel within their best friendships, although none use that word, specifically. Each seems to feel not just known, but accepted for who she is. As Liz says of Susan: "It's like she knows me too well to judge me. The judgments have already been made." Similarly, Nancy accepts her friends for who they are. She acknowledges the ways in which they are different from her, but does not try to change them.

Through their in-depth interviewing of over a hundred women, Belenky and colleagues came to understand that women have varying ways of knowing.[15] Although they focused primarily on the ways in which women learn about and make sense of the world, the authors acknowledged that particularly for the group of women they referred to as "connected knowers," the ways in which they gather and perceive information is deeply related to the ways in which they learn about and understand people. It is likely that most or all of the participants in the current study would fall at least partly into the connected knowers group, as defined by Belenky and colleagues.

Like Jordan, Belenky and colleagues spoke to the importance of empathy and understanding differences:

> Connected knowers develop procedures for gaining access to other people's knowledge. At the heart of these procedures is the capacity for empathy. Since knowledge comes from experience, the only way they can hope to understand another person's ideas is to try to share the experience that has led the person to form the idea.[16]

At first, these women are interested in learning about others' lives. Over time, however, they begin to integrate how those other people think. "Connected knowers learn through empathy."[17]

Belenky and colleagues explained that connected knowers often seek out the differences in others to learn more about the world and to experience, in some way, what others have experienced. But these women also strive to know their friends so that they may take better care of them (see Gilligan, 1982; Jordan et al., 1991; Noddings, 1984, for in-depth discussions of care)[18]: "Connected knowers make it their responsibility to understand how their friends feel and to help them think the problem through."[19] Belenky and colleagues certainly seemed to be describing many of the participants' best friendships.

As a final note to her chapter, Jordan wrote: "Mutual relationships in which one feels heard, seen, understood, and known, as well as listening, seeing, understanding, and emotionally available [sic], are vitally important to most people's psychological well-being."[20] The women who participated in my study would agree, as no doubt would countless other women who rue their male partner's inability or lack of desire to participate in just such a mutuality. Fortunately, women have other women to take on that enormously important role. "Knowing" and "Being Known" is a complex, unruly, intractable theme in women's best friendships—but we should expect nothing less after recognizing the significance it has in our lives.

Chapter 12

Conclusion

In Mary Gordon's novel *Final Payments,* Isabel ends up doing what so many of my participants can barely imagine: She dials her best friend's number when she reaches a depth from which she can find no way out on her own:

> And the miracle was that Eleanor answered the phone. There was her voice: clear, and delicate, and full of love, as if she had been waiting. . . .
>
> "Eleanor, I have to ask you what I have no right to ask you. Can you come up here now? Tonight. I need your help. I have to get out of here now. I'm afraid to wait; I'm afraid if I don't go now I'll die here."
>
> Eleanor's response was instantaneous, as if she had been preparing for months to respond to what I had only just now known I wanted to say.
>
> "I'll be there tonight."[1]

Up until the moment that Isabel made that call, she did not know she would ever do so. But somewhere in her, she had a certainty that Eleanor would respond just as she did. And it was that knowledge that enabled Isabel to raise her head just a bit from the depths of her despair and envision a way out. And it was her trust in her friend that enabled her to let go of her pride and allow Eleanor (along with Isabel's other best friend, Liz) to rescue her.

I read Mary Gordon's book for the first time some fifteen years ago. It had such great resonance for me that I made it the basis for my master's thesis in literature. When I read the novel again more recently it had new resonance. The passage I quoted never ceases to move me. It is, in many ways, my own imagined fairy tale. One much closer to the realities of my life than Sleeping Beauty and her prince. Eleanor and Liz are Isabel's princes, coming to save the damsel in distress. Isabel knows on whom she can count—not her lover, whom Isabel knows she cannot call until she loses weight and gets a better haircut; not the priest who loves Isabel, but who cries when she wants him to hear her confession because he doesn't want to hear what she has done wrong; and not her father, whose life and death have propelled Isabel into her current emotional distress. Isabel reaches out to the two people she knows will come:

> How I loved them for their solidity, for their real and possible existences, nonetheless a miracle. For they had come the moment I had called them, and they were here beside me in the fragile and exhilarating chill of the first dawn.[2]

Women believe in the solidity of their closest friendships. They count on it—and who knows what paths in life that faith allows them to take. But these friendships are far more than safety nets. They are relationships woven into the very fabric of women's lives. Their daily lives may more often than not be taken up with the demands of those whose needs are most immediate—their children, their lovers, their parents—but that in no way diminishes the value of their friendships. In fact, these friendships are often seen as an oasis in the midst of the chaos and pressures of that everyday life. I can think of the look that crosses an acquaintance's face—a mother, like me, of young children—as I tell her that I am going out that evening to have dinner with a close friend. I see a twinkling in the eye as she imagines such a luxury for herself—and a touch of envy, of course.

There is something of a guilty pleasure in the time I carve out to be with my best friends. It is unbelievable how difficult it is to find a block of time to fit each schedule. As the day approaches—often weeks after the date was first made—I excitedly anticipate it. If it must be canceled—because of illness, weather, the demands of work or children—my disappointment is palpable. I must continue on a few weeks more without my fix. It will be some more time until I can luxuriate in a few hours spent talking, laughing, relaxing in a way I can with no one else.

But there is a *however.* Fairly tales are fantasy, and thus to some extent, this is a fantasy too. Or, perhaps better, an idealization. I have an absolute belief that my best friends will be there if I need them—unless they cannot be. It may be that at the moment that I make that call that Isabel made, they will not be home. Or maybe they just will not be able to get away. I have no doubt that they will want to come to my rescue, but it simply may not be possible. Or, maybe, they will not gather the enormity of the situation, the extent to which I need them, because I will not find a way to articulate that need.

In fairy tales, the prince somehow knows both that he is needed and where to find his soon-to-be princess. The personalities of the characters—short of goodness and beauty—matter not at all. It is silly even to consider how the dynamics of the relationship factor in. Needless to say, personalities and relationship dynamics among real individuals cannot be factored out. The fantasy is rarely the reality. Sometimes my friends and I get irritated with each other. Sometimes we read signs poorly because we are not particularly attuned in the moment. Sometimes we neither know nor understand.

The findings presented here push our comprehension of female best friendships beyond stereotypic constructions. On the one hand, these relationships have been denigrated within a culture that, as evidenced by all forms of media, values the male-female lover relationship above all others. The most common happy ending is still one in which the man and woman live happily ever after. This fairy tale ending in which neither is thought to need anyone but the other is pervasive. Female friendships are traditionally believed to be characterized by disloyalty because women are believed to be catty and competitive in such friendships, particularly when a man is involved. Betty and Veronica of the *Archie* comics typify this concept of the relationship.

However, there has also been a more recent emphasis on the importance of friendships among women in the face of a culture and society where men hold more power and are the standard bearers. Feminist philosophy stresses that women should be a source of empowerment and safety for each other. The importance of supporting and loving each other unconditionally is emphasized. In the popular media, the movie *Thelma and Louise* reflects such ideas. Women have therefore been exposed to scripts that on the one hand denigrate women's relationships and on the other idealize them. The reality is far more complex than either script allows for. There is a great deal of love and support in these friendships, but there are also areas of tension and difficulty.

The participants make it clear that their closest friendships are of enormous value to them. They fulfill needs that their lover relationships do not. The women more often than not derive tremendous strength from their best friendships. These stories of female best friendship support the findings of Gilligan and others that women greatly value interconnectedness.[3] Amy describes herself as being blessed for having such friendships. Deb describes the relationship as a gift. The women feel that these relationships are an integral part of their lives—not just the icing on the cake.

An increasing literature confirms the importance of female friendships.[4] These studies show that women form deep emotional intimacies with their friends. My own findings point to a defining element of that intimacy—knowing and being known. Mutual knowing grows out of a feeling of deep trust. Being known seems to provide women with a sense of validation—they are known for who they are *and* they are accepted in spite of being known. The fact that their friends can see below the surface—that they will not be fooled into believing that what they see and hear is the whole truth—apparently gives the women a sense of safety and security. That there are people out there who will not always let them get away with taking the easy way out in an interaction is a source of comfort. Perhaps we spend so much of our day presenting to the world a persona not altogether true to ourselves, that it is a great relief to know that that persona will not be accepted as reality by someone. Although the women do not always reveal all of themselves to their friends, what seems to be important is that they *feel* known—and they feel accepted for who they are.

However, there are difficulties in the friendships, as well. Aspects of the relationships are not readily reconciled with this idea of complete trust and acceptance. Despite an expressed pleasure in being known, the women do hold back parts of themselves. One perspective might suggest that the relationships are in some ways flawed: Perhaps if the women would just have greater trust and understanding, leading to a greater intimacy, these difficulties would be avoided. But there is another explanation: The deep intimacies—deriving from being known and knowing—are, in fact, the source of some of those tensions.

As we have seen, the participants express that while it is vital to know that they can depend on their friends, to actually reach out to their friends in a time of need can feel difficult, if not impossible. The question that necessarily arises is how the resistance to allowing oneself to depend on one's friends can be reconciled with the trust that characterizes these relationships. In other words, if I trust her and I want her to know me, why is it so hard for me to tell her that sometimes it feels like I can't do it on my own? I think the answer lies in feelings of vulnerability. Along with revealing oneself to another comes a sense of exposure. As intimacy develops, there is a process of letting go and giving oneself over to the other. Because the resulting vulnerability develops through trust, it is not viewed negatively. However, it may be that there is a thin line between vulnerability that feels all right because the parameters of the relationship make one feel safe and vulnerability that feels scary. That threshold of vulnerability seems to be reached for many when feelings of dependency creep in.

It may be that to acknowledge need would make many women feel *too* vulnerable—that is, a saturation point of vulnerability would be reached. For instance, Linda says that she is more apt to call Carol than to call Emily because she is less afraid that Carol will view her as needy. Linda also expresses that she and Emily have a somewhat more knowing and intimate relationship than do she and Carol. She may, thus, feel more vulnerable with Emily. While that vulnerability may add to the overall closeness she feels in the relationship, it may also be what causes Linda to avoid any feelings of dependency toward Emily. That threshold of vulnerability may be reached sooner with Emily than with any of Linda's other friends.

Competitiveness emerged as another source of tension within the friendships. Despite their protestations to the contrary, some of the participants clearly felt competitive at times, and they were obviously uncomfortable acknowledging those feelings. The discomfort they have with their competitiveness may well be exacerbated by the closeness of their relationships with their friends. The discomfort likely arises in large part from a belief that competitive feelings are anathema to the ideal of female friendship. Thus, the closeness and intimacy of these relationships causes an already uncomfortable feeling to be virtually intolerable. The women may be able to accept that they can be competitive at times, but they cannot accept that they would feel competitive with their closest friends. To do so would feel like a betrayal of the values of the friendship. To be competitive would be to buy into the script of the disloyal, untrustworthy female friend. It matters little that they would likely not act on those competitive feelings in a hurtful or destructive way. The feelings themselves are simply taboo.

An additional issue that emerges in the interplay between knowing and competitiveness is the extent to which the women allow their friends to know this part of themselves. It seems reasonable to assume that the women are not consciously revealing this aspect of themselves. However, it is likely that the process of becoming known is not an entirely conscious one. It is not a systematic and purposeful process in which individuals carefully choose everything they want their friends to know about them. Perhaps the women are giving cues to their friends that over time will allow their friends to see their competitive feelings within the relationship. In so doing, another value of being known may be served. Through their friends' knowledge, the women may learn about themselves. And through their friends' acceptance, they may come to accept themselves. Yet, it may well be that some of the women will never reveal this aspect of themselves. Linda, in particular, is both so guarded and so wary of competitiveness that it is difficult to imagine her allowing her friends to see her competitive feelings, even if she were to acknowledge them to herself.

Finally, there is an important relationship between the feelings of competitiveness and dependence. They are, I think, two sides of a coin. Both feelings are an assertion of the self within the relationship. To feel competitive with one's friend is to acknowledge that one has desires that likely run counter to one's friend's. To feel dependent on a friend is to acknowledge that one wants—or even requires—the relationship to meet certain needs. Both feelings place the self at center stage within the relationship—they are assertions of the women's individual needs. Miller and Gilligan both discuss women's difficulties in asserting their own needs and desires.[5] Miller explains that women often associate such assertions with selfishness. Thus, feelings about affirming their selves may contribute to women's discomfort regarding feeling competitive and dependent within their friendships.

So the picture is a complex one—which is not surprising, since people are complex. We may, at times, fantasize a fairy tale ending, but my guess is that the realities, while more difficult, are far better. Our lives are all the richer for the time we put into making our friendships work. Most of the women I know feel the reality of women's friendship to lie far closer to Thelma and Louise than to Betty and Veronica. They treasure, as I do, their closest female friendships and reject the notion that women cannot trust one another. But there may be a price paid for the wholehearted acceptance of one image of friendship over the other. Many women seem loath to acknowledge that difficulties do exist in their closest friendships. They often defend against the notion that there might be some truth to the traditional stereotype. That is, they fear that if they allow for the possibility that there are aspects of their friendships that do not work all that well, they will provide support for that negative image of female friendships. There also seems to be guilt at the idea that they cannot attain an impossibly high standard. It is my hope that studies such as this one that allow the many dimensions of these relationships to be revealed will enable women to accept that their friendships can be less than perfect, yet still wonderfully supportive and caring.

Appendix A

Transcript versus Poem

Transcript

N: Um, I think . . . Lisa is loyal in her own way, like . . . she's not . . . while all this is going on . . . like she's not turning her back.

P: OK.

N: Like you can see it in her face, that she's connected and that she doesn't know what to do. Like she's trying to find a way. Um . . . Lisa is real loyal. It—it's—it—you know I guess in combination with those—with the other things I said, it—you, you would think that she wasn't loyal. Um . . . you know, she's not someone who would ever lie, or she's not under-handed, she doesn't gossip, like she's a very good friend, but she gets tied up, at—at least from my perception, she might perceive it very differently.

Poem

> Um
> I think
> Lisa is loyal
> in her own way
> like
> she's not
> while all this is going on
> like she's not
> turning her back.
>
> OK.
>
> Like you an see it in her face
> that she's connected

and that she doesn't know what to do.
Like she's trying to find a way.
Um
Lisa is real loyal
It—it's—it you know I guess in
combination with those
with those other things I said
it—you, you would think that she wasn't loyal.
Um
you know, she's not someone who would ever lie
or she's not underhanded
she doesn't gossip
like she's a very good friend
but she gets tied up
at—at least from my perception
she might perceive it very differently.

Appendix B

Nancy Poem 1

1 I guess like in a nut
2 shell
3 what happened was
4 I was
5 a supervisor.
6 Um
7 and Lisa—
8 this woman Doreen also
9 you know
10 I hired her and she also worked with us.
11 Um
12 what had happened is Doreen
13 had a lot of problems at work.
14 What Doreen basically did
15 is she wedged herself
16 between Lisa and myself.
17 And Lisa got sucked into it
18 and
19 she
20 uh
21 she
22 she a—
23 from my perspective
24 she aligned herself with Doreen
25 and actually I think from her perspective
26 she'd say the same thing she pulled very much away from me
27 and towards Doreen.
28 Um
29 I forget
30 what the incident was

31 where, actually
32 well
33 wh—what—some
34 what happened
35 was
36 there's some incident
37 where Doreen looked really horrible.
38 And
39 it was very clear
40 that I had
41 you know
42 that this was not
43 like
44 some kinda interpersonal relationship
45 problem between
46 Doreen and me
47 that everybody else could wipe their hands clean of
48 as like
49 you know
50 "it's just their problem
51 and we can be friends with both
52 and I can pull away from her
53 because I w—"
54 it was very clear
55 that Doreen
56 had done something awful.
57 And that
58 I had done nothing.

59 YOU MEAN THAT IT WAS VERY CLEAR TO EVERYONE—

60 —it was very clear to everybody.
61 And it was very clear to Lisa
62 that
63 her pulling away from me and toward Li—
64 you know she
65 she, she was actually able
66 you know
67 she actually told me that
68 Um
69 that
70 she was wrong.

71 And that
72 you know
73 ba—you know
74 basic—you know
75 our friendship was
76 hurt by that
77 Um
78 but you know a piece of that is just Lisa
79 Lisa gets torn
80 um
81 Doreen
82 at that time
83 Doreen is a
84 you know
85 she is a very wealthy woman
86 who basically
87 in many ways
88 bought Lisa.
89 She
90 invited her places
91 that Lisa
92 didn't want to turn down.
93 So she was
94 "what should I do here?
95 You know
96 she has all these
97 you know she's very wealthy and I can go here
98 or I can
99 do this."
100 Um
101 and she—
102 she got to see it
103 um
104 and actually e—even—
105 I guess
106 I guess
107 the last time she brought up Doreen
108 was last year.
109 She is—she—
110 my guess is she's still
111 there's still stuff there.
112 But I don't

113 talk about it.
114 Like she'll bring it up.
115 She'll want—
116 she in many ways wants me
117 to like Doreen
118 And I never will.
119 You know, I
120 could tolerate her
121 and be at a party with her
122 but
123 do I want to go to a dinner party and sit next to her?
124 Fat chance in hell.
125 Um
126 but Lisa would like that
127 so she'll bring it up
128 to see
129 my end
130 what my perception is
131 to see
132 what I'm thinking.
133 And to see if that's all over with
134 and she can forget about it

135 NOW WHY WOULD SHE WANT YOU TO LIKE DOREEN?

136 Well
137 I guess
138 I guess it just—
139 you know like there are some things
140 that
141 she
142 would like—
143 like at Lisa's wedding
144 we both were there together.
145 Um
146 and I guess some other things
147 it would just make her life
148 I don't know
149 for inst—
150 at this particular point
151 like 1997
152 I don't think it makes all that much difference

153 because our paths
154 I don't think
155 I can't think of any good reasons for them to cross
156 If she had a party
157 Doreen and I both might go.
158 it honestly wouldn't be an issue for me.
159 That actually still might be an issue for Lisa.
160 You know when I think about that
161 when I think about Lisa had a par—
162 there was a party for Lisa
163 not so long ago
164 Doreen didn't go
165 but my guess is
166 that would have been on Lisa's mind.

Appendix C

Nancy Poem 2

1 AND I WAS JUST WONDERING HOW THAT LOYALTY IN YOUR MIND
  MANIF—

2 How does it manifest itself
3 like while I'm saying, saying what I'm saying about Lisa.
4 Um
5 I think
6 Lisa is loyal
7 in her own way
8 like
9 she's not
10 while all this is going on
11 like she's not
12 turning her back.

13 OK.

14 Like you can see it in her face
15 that she's connected
16 and that she doesn't know what to do.
17 Like she's trying to find a way.
18 Um
19 Lisa is real loyal
20 It—it's—it—you know I guess in
21 combination with those
22 with those other things I said
23 it—you, you would think that she wasn't
24 loyal.
25 Um
26 you know, she's not someone who would ever lie

27   or
28   she's not underhanded
29   she doesn't gossip
30   like she's a very good friend
31   but she gets tied up
32   at—at least from my perception
33   she might perceive it very differently.
34   Um
35   you know
36   wh—when there are competing things.
37   But not like she just
38   walks away.

39   OK.

40   Like she's like—
41   you can see her stuck there.
42   Though
43   she may
44   you know
45   like with Doreen
46   you know I knew
47   the whole time this was going on
48   that this was very difficult for her.
49   I wasn't going to save her from it.
50   'Cause this was
51   like
52   her stuff
53   not my stuff.
54   Um
55   but like she just didn't
56   like some people could just like
57   drop you and not think.
58   And like not be connected.
59   She never I—I—
60   she never was like that.

61   SO HOW WOULD YOU DEFINE LOYALTY—

62   —how would I define loyalty?

63   —IN A FRIENDSHIP?

64 Um
65 I don't know
66 I guess like, well—
67 loyalty is
68 I don't know
69 like in a friend
70 it's someone who is always your friend no matter what.
71 Um
72 and it's someone
73 who
74 will
75 stand by you no matter what.
76 Um
77 I guess what I'm saying about Lisa
78 is she'll s—
79 she does
80 stand by you no matter what
81 but within her limitations.

82 OK.

83 And I think
84 over time
85 those limitations have lessened.
86 Hopefully over
87 time
88 you know, like
89 over life
90 they'll continue to lessen with
91 more life.
92 And I think they have
93 you know.
94 How she
95 is now
96 is very different
97 than how she was
98 seven or eight years ago.
99 And that was real—
100 the incident with Doreen was
101 mmm
102 years ago
103 years ago.

104   AH HAH.

105   A long time ago.

106   OK.

107   WHAT ABOUT WITH CLAUDIA? SH—

108   Claudia
109   will be my friend
110   till the day I die
111   or the day she dies.
112   Um
113   Claudia
114   Claudia's a very loyal friend.
115   Um
116   She's someone
117   that
118   I know is always there
119   Um she's not someone
120   who
121   I don't know, she's
122   she would always be my friend.
123   Like I don't—
124   you know, I don't know
125   there's a greater distance
126   um
127   spacewise, like she's not someone
128   who
129   I could go—you know, actually I could.
130   I could go visit her any time I wanted to.
131   And that would be fine.
132   It's not something
133   that I would do.
134   And Lisa's also the same way.
135   I could call Lisa
136   and
137   I could see either one of them
138   whenever I wanted to.
139   Like if I needed
140   help.
141   I could count on both of them.

142 Um
143 not that I would.
144 But I could
145 And
146 you know
147 I feel the same way towards them.
148 That I wouldn't think twice
149 about doing something for them.

150 OK. SO IT'S A TRAIT THAT YOU FEEL THAT YOU HAVE, AS WELL.

151 Yeah. Towards them?

152 YEAH.

153 Yes, you know yes.
154 Well I think
155 in general
156 I think I'm a very loyal person.
157 But I think
158 when you talk about loyalty in friendship
159 um
160 there's a depth to that
161 that you have
162 with different people.
163 You know, like
164 um
165 there are many people
166 you know
167 I would say
168 I very much care about and am being loyal to
169 but under certain circumstances
170 if I hadda choose
171 I'd be conflicted
172 about how much I have to give
173 But then there's a group of people
174 who
175 it doesn't matter
176 how much I have to give
177 'cause that's what I need to do
178 because they're my
179 very good friends.

Appendix D

Liz Poem

1 I think
2 I think there are
3 there are a couple times when they made really bad decisions
4 and I was thinking,
5 "Wow this is a really bad decision,"
6 but I haven't necessarily
7 said anything about it
8 because either
9 it was done
10 and there's no point of like
11 pouring salt in the wound and saying,
12 "Well, that was really
13 you know, stupid."
14 So it was either done
15 or it was something that I felt like
16 they felt strongly about
17 I don't agree with
18 but there's nothing I can do.
19 Like actually right now
20 Susan's cousin
21 just moved in with her
22 and I think this is like a *disaster.*
23 I think it's *terrible.*
24 But I really don't feel like I can say to her
25 "This is *terrible*" (she laughs ironically).
26 Although I
27 I absolutely feel that way.

28 DO YOU THINK SHE KNOWS THAT, THAT YOU WOULD THINK THAT?

29   Oh, she knows I think it.

30   YEAH, THAT'S WHAT I WOULD—

31   She—
32   I don't have a good relationship with her cousin.
33   He has a *terrible* track record. And
34   you know, my feeling is
35   that he's done some things that
36   as far as I'm concerned are not forgivable.
37   I will not
38   ever
39   have any type of
40   relationship with him
41   ever.
42   But she—
43   of course it's her cousin
44   so she's
45   a little bit more forgiving
46   than I am. But
47   he just moved in with her and I think it's
48   I think it's *terrible*.
49   And she's getting married
50   and he's living there
51   it's just terri—
52   and he's an alcoholic
53   and he has an alcoholic wife
54   I mean it's like—

55   OH THEY ALL MOVED IN?

56   They *all* moved in
57   to her new house.
58   Yeah
59   it's terr—
60   I think it's terrible.
61   And I also know how Susan is with him.
62   And how she really
63   she's very protective of him
64   And how she just
65   takes
66   abuse from him

67 because she feels the need to
68 protect him
69 because he has a serious problem.
70 And
71 I think it's really terrible.
72 And she knows that I—
73 she kno—
74 she knows that I'm thinking this
75 but I haven't
76 said to her
77 "Susan this is a terrible mistake."
78 Because
79 I just think that it's (she sighs)
80 you know it's happening regardless
81 and I think
82 she's in some ways
83 I mean I think she
84 has so many issues
85 with her cousin
86 that
87 I think it would just make things worse if I
88 you know said to her
89 "This is
90 this is terrible."
91 Because I think she probably knows it
92 but I don't think wants to believe it.
93 So
94 I mean and who knows
95 maybe it'll work out.
96 But
97 I'm not bettin' on it (she laughs ironically).
98 So that is
99 a prime example of something I really feel like I cannot
100 say
101 anything to her about.

102 OK.

103 So
104 although she knows it.

Notes

Preface

1. Virginia Woolf, *A Room of One's Own.* San Diego: Harcourt Brace, 1989. (Original work published 1929), p. 82.

Chapter 1

1. Carmen Renee Berry and Tamara Traeder, *Girlfriends: Invisible Bonds.* Berkeley, CA: Wildcat Canyon, 1995.
2. Helen Gouldner and Mary S. Strong, *Speaking of Friendship: Middle-Class Women and Their Friends.* New York: Greenwood, 1987, pp. 105-106.
3. Fern L. Johnson and Elizabeth Aries, "The Talk of Women Friends." *Women's Studies International Forum* 6(1983): 353-361.
4. Stacey J. Oliker, *Best Friends and Marriage: Exchange Among Women.* Berkeley: University of California, 1989.
5. Virginia Woolf, *A Room of One's Own.* San Diego: Harcourt Brace, 1989. (Original work published 1929), p. 82.
6. Ibid., p. 83.
7. Mary Gordon, "Women's Friendships," *Redbook,* July 1976.
8. Ibid., p. 162.
9. Toni Morrison, *Sula.* San Diego: Plume, 1973, pp. 120-121.
10. Ibid., p. 174.
11. Woolf, *A Room of One's Own.*
12. Jacqueline S. Weinstock and Esther D. Rothblum, Eds., *Lesbian Friendships: For Ourselves and Each Other.* New York: New York University, 1996.
13. Daphne Patai, "Constructing a Self." *Feminist Studies,* 14(1988): 47.
14. Paul Atkinson, *Understanding Ethnographic Texts.* Newbury Park, CA: Sage, 1992, p. 6.

Chapter 4

1. Helen Gouldner and Mary S. Strong, *Speaking of Friendship: Middle-Class Women and Their Friends.* New York: Greenwood, 1987.

Chapter 5

1. Mary Catherine Ford, "Competition Among Women at Work." PhD dissertation, California School of Professional Psychology, 1987; Constance A. Johannessen, "Competition Between Women: A Conceptualization and an Evaluation of the Relational Process." PhD dissertation, Antioch University, New England Graduate School, 1992.

2. Janet Lever, "Sex Differences in Games Children Play." *Social Problems* 23(1976): 478-487; Martina Horner, "Toward an Understanding of Achievement-Related Conflicts in Women." *Journal of Social Issues* 28(1972): 157-175; Georgia Sassen, "Success Anxiety in Women: A Constructivist Interpretation of its Source and its Significance." *Harvard Educational Review* 50(1980): 13-24.

3. Lever, "Sex Differences in Games, " p. 478.

4. Ibid., p. 482.

5. Ibid., p. 483.

6. Ibid., p. 485.

7. Ibid., p. 484.

8. Horner, "Toward an Understanding"; Sassen, "Success Anxiety in Women."

9. Horner, "Toward an Understanding."

10. Sassen, "Success Anxiety in Women," p. 18.

11. Ibid., p. 18.

12. Nancy Chodorow, *The Reproduction of Mothering.* Berkeley: University of California, 1978; Carol Gilligan, *In a Different Voice: Psychological Theory and Women's Development.* Cambridge, MA: Harvard University, 1982.

13. Sassen, "Success Anxiety in Women," p. 19.

14. Chodorow, *The Reproduction of Mothering;* Gilligan, *In a Different Voice;* Judith V. Jordan, Alexandra G. Kaplan, Jean B. Miller, Irene P. Stiver, and Janet L. Surrey, Eds., *Women's Growth in Connection: Writings from the Stone Center,* New York: Guilford, 1991; Nona P. Lyons, "Two Perspectives: On Self, Relationships, and Morality." *Harvard Educational Review* 53(1983): 125-145.

15. See Gilligan, *In a Different Voice;* and see Nel Noddings, *Caring: A Feminine Approach to Ethics and Moral Education,* Berkeley: University of California, 1984.

16. Johannessen, "Competition Between Women," p. 37.

17. Lever, "Sex Differences in Games."

18. See Chodorow, *The Reproduction of Mothering;* see Gilligan, *In a Different Voice;* and see Jordan et al., *Women's Growth in Connection."*

19. Ford, "Competition Among Women at Work."

20. Valerie Miner, "Rumours from the Cauldron: Competition Among Feminist Writers." *Women's Studies International Forum* 8(1988): 45-50.

21. Ibid., p. 46.

22. See also Sharon Griffin-Pierson, "Achievement and Competitiveness in Women." *Journal of College Student Development* 29(1988): 491-495; and see also Christine E. Meyer-Pfaff, "The Link Between Competition and Human Relationships: Women Athletes Speak of Competition and Cooperation." PhD dissertation, Seattle University, 1990.

23. Meyer-Pfaff, "The Link Between Competition and Human Relationships," p. 158.

Chapter 8

1. Carol Gilligan, *In a Different Voice: Psychological Theory and Women's Development.* Cambridge, MA: Harvard University, 1982.

2. Irene P. Stiver, "The Meanings of 'Dependency' in Female-Male Relationships," in *Women's Growth in Connection: Writings from the Stone Center,* Eds. Judith V. Jordan, Alexandra G. Kaplan, Jean B. Miller, Irene P. Stiver, and Janet L. Surrey (New York: Guilford, pp. 143-161), 1991, p. 147.

3. Ibid., p. 143.

4. Nel Noddings, *Caring: A Feminine Approach to Ethics and Moral Education.* Berkeley: University of California, 1984.

5. Gilligan, *In a Different Voice,* p. 17.

Chapter 11

1. Gordon J. Chelune, *Self-Disclosure: Origins, Patterns, and Implications of Openness in Interpersonal Relationships.* San Francisco: Jossey-Bass, 1979.

2. Mary F. Belenky, Blythe M. Clinchy, Nancy R. Goldberger, and Jill M. Turule, *Women's Ways of Knowing: The Development of Self, Voice, and Mind.* New York: Basic Books, 1986; Gordon J. Chelune, J. T. Robison, and M.J. Kommor, "A Cognitive Interactional Model of Intimate Relationships," in *Communication, Intimacy, and Close Relationships,* Ed. Valerian J. Derlega (Orlando: Academic, pp. 11-40), 1984; Judith V. Jordan, "Empathy and Self Boundaries," in *Women's Growth in Connection: Writings from the Stone Center,* Eds. Judith V. Jordan, Alexandra G. Kaplan, Jean B. Miller, Irene P. Stiver, and Janet L. Surrey (New York: Guilford, pp. 67-80), 1991.

3. Chelune et al., "A Cognitive Interactional Model," p. 14.

4. Ibid., p. 16.

5. Ibid.

6. Ibid.

7. Ibid.

8. Jordan, "Empathy and Self Boundaries."

9. Ibid., p. 83.

10. Ibid., p. 86.

11. Ibid.

12. Ibid., p. 88.

13. Ibid., p. 89.

14. Ibid.

15. Belenky et al., *Women's Ways of Knowing.*

16. Ibid., p. 113.

17. Ibid., p. 115.

18. For in-depth discussions of care, see Carol Gilligan, *In a Different Voice: Psychological Theory and Women's Development.* Cambridge, MA: Harvard University, 1982; Judith V. Jordan et al., Eds., *Women's Growth in Connection;* and Nel Noddings, *Caring: A Feminine Approach to Ethics and Moral Education,* Berkeley: University of California, 1984.

19. Belenky et al., *Women's Ways of Knowing,* p. 120.

20. Jordan, "Empathy and Self Boundaries," p. 96.

Chapter 12

1. Mary Gordon, *Final Payments.* New York: Random House, 1978, p. 247.

2. Ibid., p. 250.

3. Nancy Chodorow, *The Reproduction of Mothering,* Berkeley: University of California, 1978; Carol Gilligan, *In a Different Voice: Psychological Theory and Women's Development.* Cambridge, MA: Harvard University, 1982; Mary F. Belenky, Blythe M. Clinchy, Nancy R. Goldberger, and Jill M. Turule, *Women's Ways of Knowing: The Development of Self, Voice, and Mind.* New York: Basic Books, 1986; Judith V. Jordan, Alexandra G. Kaplan, Jean B. Miller, Irene P. Stiver, and Janet L. Surrey, Eds., *Women's Growth in Connection: Writings from the Stone Center.* New York: Guilford, 1991; Nona P. Lyons, "Two Perspectives: On Self, Relationships, and Morality." *Harvard Educational Review* 53(1983): 125-145.

4. Carol S. Becker, "Friendship Between Women: A Phenomenological Study of Best Friends." *Journal of Phenomenological Psychology* 18(1987): 59-72; Belenky et al., *Women's Ways of Knowing*; Carmen R. Berry and Tamara Traeder, *Girlfriends: Enduring Ties.* Berkeley: Wildcat Canyon, 1995; Stephanie Beukema, "Women's Best Friendships: Their Meaning and Meaningfulness," PhD dissertation, Harvard University, 1990; Luise Eichenbaum and Susie Orbach, *Between Women: Love, Envy, and Competition in Women's Friendships.* New York: Viking, 1988; Helen Gouldner and Mary S. Strong, *Speaking of Friendship: Middle-Class Women and Their Friends.* New York: Greenwood, 1987; Fern L. Johnson and Elizabeth Aries, "The Talk of Women Friends." *Women's Studies International Forum* 6(1983): 353-361; Pat O'Conner, *Friendships Between Women: A Critical Review.* New York: Guilford, 1992; Stacey J. Oliker, *Best Friends and Marriage: Exchange Among Women.* Berkeley: University of California, 1989.

5. Gilligan, *In a Different Voice*; Jean B. Miller, "Women and Power," in *Women's Growth in Connection: Writings from the Stone Center,* Eds. Jordan et al. (New York: Guilford, 1991, pp. 197-205), 1991.

Bibliography

Atkinson, P. *Understanding Ethnographic Texts.* Newbury Park, CA: Sage, 1992.

Austen, J. *Pride and Prejudice.* New York: Bantam, 1981. (Original work published 1813.)

Becker, C. S. "Friendship Between Women: A Phenomenological Study of Best Friends." *Journal of Phenomenological Psychology* 18(1981): 59-72.

Belenky, M. F., Clinchy, B. M., Goldberger, N. R., and Tarule, J. M. *Women's Ways of Knowing: The Development of Self, Voice, and Mind.* New York: Basic Books, 1986.

Berg, J. H. "Development of Friendship Between Roommates." *Journal of Personality and Social Psychology* 46(1984): 346-356.

Berg, J. H. and Archer, R. L. "Disclosure or Concern: A Second Look at Liking for the Norm Breaker." *Journal of Personality* 48(1984): 245-257.

Berry, C. R. and Traeder, T. *Girlfriends: Invisible Bonds, Enduring Ties.* Berkeley, CA: Wildcat Canyon, 1995.

Beukema, S. "Women's Best Friendships: Their Meaning and Meaningfulness." PhD Dissertation, Harvard University, 1990.

Block, J. D. and Greenberg, D. *Women and Friendship.* New York: Franklin Watts, 1985.

Bogdan, R. C. and Biklen, S. K. *Qualitative Research for Education: An Introduction to Theory and Methods.* Boston: Allyn and Bacon, 1992.

Brightman, C. *Between Friends: The Correspondence of Hannah Arendt and Mary McCarthy, 1949-1975.* New York: Harcourt Brace, 1995.

Brontë, C. *Jane Eyre.* Oxford: Oxford University, 1975. (Original work published 1847.)

Bruner, J. *Acts of Meaning.* Cambridge, MA: Harvard, 1990.

Bruner, J. *Actual Minds, Possible Worlds.* Cambridge, MA: Harvard, 1986.

Caldwell, M.A. and Peplau, L.A. "Sex Differences in Same-Sex Friendship." *Sex Roles* 8(1982): 721-732.

Chelune, G. J., Ed. *Self-Disclosure: Origins, Patterns, and Implications of Openness in Interpersonal Relationships.* San Francisco: Jossey-Bass, 1979.

Chelune, G. J., Robison, J. T., and Kommor, M. J. "A Cognitive Interactional Model of Intimate Relationships." In *Communication, Intimacy, and Close Relationships,* Ed. V. J. Derlega (Orlando: Academic), pp. 81-96, 1984.

Chodorow, N. "Family Structure and Feminine Personality." In *Woman, Culture, and Society,* Eds. M. Z. Rosaldo and L. Lamphere (Stanford: Stanford University Press), pp. 43-66, 1974.

Chodorow, N. *The Reproduction of Mothering.* Berkeley: University of California, 1978.

Daly, M., Ed. *Surface Tension: Love, Sex, and Politics Between Lesbians and Straight Women.* New York: Simon & Schuster, 1996.

Davidson, L. R. and Duberman, L. "Friendship: Communication and Interactional Patterns in Same-Sex Dyads." *Sex Roles* 8(1982): 809-822.

Derlega, V. J. and Chaikin, A. L. "Privacy and Self-Disclosure in Social Relationships." *Journal of Social Issues* 33(1977): 102-115.

Derlega, V. J., Durham, B., Gockel, B., and Sholis, D. "Sex differences in Self-Disclosure: Effects of Topic Content, Friendship, and Partner's Sex." *Sex Roles* 7(1981): 433-447.

Duck, S. and Wright, P. "Reexamining Gender Differences in Same-Gender Friendships: A Close Look at Two Kinds of Data." *Sex Roles* 28(1993): 709-727.

Eichenbaum, L. and Orbach, S. *Between Women: Love, Envy, and Competition in Women's Friendships.* New York: Viking, 1988.

Elkins, L. E. and Peterson, C. "Gender Differences in Best Friendships." *Sex Roles* 29(1993): 497-508.

Ely, M., Anzul, M., Friedman, T., Garner, D., and Steinmetz, A. M. *Doing Qualitative Research: Circles Within Circles.* London: Falmer, 1991.

Ely, M., Vinz, R., Downing, M., and Anzul, M. *On Writing Qualitative Research: Living by Words.* London: Falmer, 1997.

Erikson, E. H. *Childhood and Society.* New York: W.W. Norton, 1985. (Original work published 1950.)

Faderman, L. *Surpassing the Love of Men: Romantic Friendship and Love Between Women from the Renaissance to the Present.* New York: William Morrow, 1981.

Ford, M. C. "Competition Among Women at Work." PhD dissertation, California School of Professional Psychology, 1987.

Gilligan, C. *In a Different Voice: Psychological Theory and Women's Development.* Cambridge, MA: Harvard, 1982.

Gitter, A. G. and Black, H. "Is Self-Disclosure Self-Revealing?" *Journal of Counseling Psychology* 23(1976): 327-332.

Glaser, B. D. and Strauss, A. K. *The Discovery of Grounded Theory.* Chicago: Aldine, 1967.

Gordon, M. "Women's Friendships." *Redbook,* July 1976.

Gouldner, H. and Strong, M. S. *Speaking of Friendship: Middle-Class Women and Their Friends.* New York: Greenwood Press, 1987.

Griffin-Pierson, S. "Achievement and Competitiveness in Women." *Journal of College Student Development* 29(1988): 491-495.

Guba, E. and Lincoln, Y. *Fourth Generation Evaluation.* Newbury Park, CA: Sage, 1989.

Hays, R. B. "A Longitudinal Study of Friendship Development." *Journal of Personality and Social Psychology* 48(1985): 900-924.

Hays, R. B. "The Day-to-Day Functioning of Close Versus Casual Friendships." *Journal of Social and Personal Relationships* 6(1989): 21-37.

Heilbrun, C. G. *Writing a Woman's Life.* New York: Ballantine, 1988.

Horner, M. "Toward an Understanding of Achievement-Related Conflicts in Women." *Journal of Social Issues* 28(1972): 157-175.

Howard, G. S. "A Narrative Approach to Thinking, Cross-Cultural Psychology, and Psychotherapy." *American Psychologist* 46(1991): 187-197.

Irigary, L. *This Sex Which Is Not One.* Trans. C. Porter. Ithaca, NY: Cornell, 1985. (Original work published 1977.)

Johannessen, C. A. "Competition Between Women: A Conceptualization and an Evaluation of the Relational Process." PhD dissertation, Antioch University, New England Graduate School, 1992.

Johnson, F. L. and Aries, E. J. "The Talk of Women Friends." *Women's Studies International Forum* 6(1983): 353-361.

Jordan, J. V. "Empathy and Self Boundaries." In *Women's Growth in Connection: Writings from the Stone Center,* Eds. J. V. Jordan, A. G. Kaplan, J. B. Miller, I. P. Stiver, and J. L. Surrey (New York: Guilford), pp. 67-80, 1991.

Jordan, J. V. The Meaning of Mutuality. In *Women's Growth in Connection: Writings from the Stone Center,* Eds. J. V. Jordan, A. G. Kaplan, J. B. Miller, I. P. Stiver, and J. L. Surrey (New York: Guilford), pp. 81-96, 1991.

Jordan, J. V., Kaplan, A. G., Miller, J. B., Stiver, I. P., and Surrey, J. L. Eds. *Women's Growth in Connection: Writings from the Stone Center.* New York: Guilford, 1991.

Lever, J. "Sex Differences in the Games Children Play." *Social Problems* 23(1976): 478-487.

Lincoln, Y. S. and Guba, E. G. *Naturalistic Inquiry.* Beverly Hills, CA: Sage, 1985.

Lindenbaum, J. "The Shattering of an Illusion: Towards the Development of Competition in Lesbian Relationships." Unpublished manuscript, University of California, Berkeley, 1983.

Lyons, N. P. Two Perspectives: On Self, Relationships, and Morality. *Harvard Educational Review* 53(1983): 125-145.

McAdams, D. P. "Unity and Purpose in Human Lives: The Emergence of Identity as a Life Story." In *Studying Persons and Lives,* Eds. A. I. Rabin, R. A. Zucker, R. A. Emmons, and S. Frank (New York: Springer), pp. 148-200, 1990.

Meyer-Pfaff, C. E. "The Link Between Competition and Human Relationships: Women Athletes Speak of Competition and Cooperation." PhD dissertation, Seattle University, 1990.

Miller, J. B. "The Development of Women's Sense of Self." In *Women's Growth in Connection: Writings from the Stone Center,* Eds. J. V. Jordan, A. G. Kaplan, J. B. Miller, I. P. Stiver, and J. L. Surrey (New York: Guilford), pp. 11-26, 1991.

Miller, J. B. "Women and Power." In *Women's Growth in Connection: Writings from the Stone Center,* Eds. J. V. Jordan, A. G. Kaplan, J. B. Miller, I. P. Stiver, and J. L. Surrey (New York: Guilford), pp. 197-205, 1991.

Miner, V. "Rumours from the Cauldron: Competition Among Feminist Writers." *Women's Studies International Forum* 8(1985): 45-50.

Morrison, T. *Sula.* New York: Plume, 1973.

Noddings, N. *Caring: A Feminine Approach to Ethics and Moral Education.* Berkeley: University of California, 1984.

O'Connor, P. *Friendships Between Women: A Critical Review.* New York: Guilford, 1992.

Oliker, S. J. *Best Friends and Marriage: Exchange Among Women.* Berkeley: University of California Press, 1989.

Patai, D. Constructing a Self. *Feminist Studies* 14(1988): 143-165.

Payant, K. "Female Friendship in the Contemporary *Bildungsroman.*" In *Communication and Women's Friendships: Parallels and Intersections in Literature and Life,* Eds. J. D. Ward and J. S. Mink (Bowling Green, OH: Bowling Green State University Popular Press), pp. 151-163, 1993.

Raymond, J. G. *A Passion for Friends: Toward a Philosophy of Female Affection.* Boston: Beacon Press, 1986.

Reisman, J. M. "Intimacy in Same-Sex Friendships." *Sex Roles* 23(1990): 65-82.

Rich, A. "Compulsory Heterosexuality and Lesbian Existence." In *The Lesbian and Gay Studies Reader,* Eds. H. Abelove, M. A. Barale, and D. M. Halperin (New York: Routledge), pp. 227-254, 1993.

Rose, S. M. "Same- and Cross-Sex Friendships and the Psychology of Homosociality." *Sex Roles* 12(1985): 63-74.

Rose, S. and Roades, L. "Feminism and Women's Friendships." *Psychology of Women Quarterly* 11(1987): 243-254.

Sassen, G. Success Anxiety in Women: A Constructivist Interpretation of Its Source and Its Significance. *Harvard Educational Review* 50(1980): 13-24.

Seidman, I. E. *Interviewing As Qualitative Research: A Guide for Researchers and Social Sciences.* New York: Teachers College, 1991.

Smith-Rosenberg, C. "The Female World of Love and Ritual: Relations Between Women in Nineteenth-Century America." *Signs* 1(1975): 1-29.

Spradley, J. *The Ethnographic Interview.* New York: Holt, Rinehart, and Winston, 1979.

Stiver, I. P. "The Meanings of 'Dependency' in Female-Male Relationships." In *Women's Growth in Connection: Writings from the Stone Center,* Eds. J. V. Jordan, A. G. Kaplan, J. B. Miller, I. P. Stiver, and J. L. Surrey (New York: Guilford), pp. 143-161, 1991.

Strauss, A. L. and Corbin, J. M. *Basics of Qualitative Research: Grounded Theory Procedures and Techniques.* Newbury Park, CA: Sage, 1990.

Surrey, J. " The 'Self-in-Relation': A Theory of Women's Development." In *Women's Growth in Connection: Writings from the Stone Center,* Eds. J. V. Jordan, A. G.

Kaplan, J. B. Miller, I. P. Stiver, and J. L. Surrey (New York: Guilford), pp. 51-66, 1991.

Tesch, R. *Qualitative Research: Analysis Types and Software Tools.* London: Falmer Press, 1990.

van Manen, M. *Researching Lived Experience.* New York: State University of New York Press, 1990.

Walker, K. "'Always There for Me': Friendship Patterns and Expectations Among Middle- and Working-Class Men and Women." *Sociological Forum* 10(1995): 273-296.

Ward, J. D. and Mink, J. S., Eds. *Communication and Women's Friendships: Parallels and Intersections in Literature and Life.* Bowling Green, OH: Bowling Green State University, 1993.

Way, N. *Everyday Courage: The Lives and Stories of Urban Teenagers (Qualitative Studies in Psychology Series).* New York: New York University, 1998.

Weinrich, J. D. *Sexual Landscapes: Why We Are What We Are. Why We Love Whom We Love.* New York: Charles Scribner's Sons, 1987.

Weinrich, J. D. "The Periodic Table Model of the Gender Transpositions: Part II. Limerent and Lusty Sexual Attractions and the Nature of Bisexuality." *The Journal of Sex Research* 24(1988): 113-129.

Weinstock, J. S. and Rothblum, E. D., Eds. *Lesbian Friendships: For Ourselves and Each Other.* New York: New York University, 1996.

Wharton, E. *The House of Mirth.* New York: Berkeley, 1984. (Original work published in 1905.)

Witherall, C. and Noddings, N., Eds. *Stories Lives Tell: Narrative and Dialogue in Education.* New York: Teachers College, Columbia University, 1991.

Woolf, V. *A Room of One's Own.* San Diego: Harcourt Brace, 1989. (Original work published 1929.)

Wright, P. H. "Men's Friendships, Women's Friendships, and the Alleged Inferiority of the Latter." *Sex Roles* 8(1982): 1-20.

Wright, P. H. and Scanlon, M. B. "Gender Role Orientations and Friendship: Some Attenuation, but Gender Differences Abound. *Sex Roles* 24(1991): 551-566.

Index

Order a copy of this book with this form or online at:
http://www.haworthpressinc.com/store/product.asp?sku=4642

WOMEN'S BEST FRIENDSHIPS
Beyond Betty, Veronica, Thelma, and Louise

_____in hardbound at $39.95 (ISBN: 0-7890-1539-0)

_____in softbound at $19.95 (ISBN: 0-7890-1540-4)

COST OF BOOKS_____

OUTSIDE USA/CANADA/
MEXICO: ADD 20%____

POSTAGE & HANDLING_____
(US: $4.00 for first book & $1.50
for each additional book)
Outside US: $5.00 for first book
& $2.00 for each additional book)

SUBTOTAL_____

in Canada: add 7% GST____

STATE TAX____
(NY, OH & MIN residents, please
add appropriate local sales tax)

FINAL TOTAL____
(If paying in Canadian funds,
convert using the current
exchange rate, UNESCO
coupons welcome.)

❏   **BILL ME LATER:** ($5 service charge will be added)
(Bill-me option is good on US/Canada/Mexico orders only;
not good to jobbers, wholesalers, or subscription agencies.)

❏ Check here if billing address is different from
shipping address and attach purchase order and
billing address information.

Signature_____

❏ **PAYMENT ENCLOSED: $_____**

❏ **PLEASE CHARGE TO MY CREDIT CARD.**

❏ Visa   ❏ MasterCard   ❏ AmEx   ❏ Discover
❏ Diner's Club   ❏ Eurocard   ❏ JCB

Account # _____

Exp. Date_____

Signature_____

Prices in US dollars and subject to change without notice.

NAME_____

INSTITUTION_____

ADDRESS_____

CITY_____

STATE/ZIP_____

COUNTRY_____ COUNTY (NY residents only)_____

TEL_____ FAX_____

E-MAIL_____

May we use your e-mail address for confirmations and other types of information? ❏ Yes ❏ No
We appreciate receiving your e-mail address and fax number. Haworth would like to e-mail or fax special
discount offers to you, as a preferred customer. **We will never share, rent, or exchange your e-mail address
or fax number.** We regard such actions as an invasion of your privacy.

Order From Your Local Bookstore or Directly From
The Haworth Press, Inc.
10 Alice Street, Binghamton, New York 13904-1580 • USA
TELEPHONE: 1-800-HAWORTH (1-800-429-6784) / Outside US/Canada: (607) 722-5857
FAX: 1-800-895-0582 / Outside US/Canada: (607) 722-6362
E-mail: getinfo@haworthpressinc.com
PLEASE PHOTOCOPY THIS FORM FOR YOUR PERSONAL USE.
www.HaworthPress.com

BOF02